YEAK
AROUND THE
WORLD

ANNE ROONEY
ILLUSTRATED BY CHARLOTTE FARMER

THIS BOOK BELONGS TO

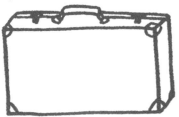

Kane Miller
A DIVISION OF EDC PUBLISHING

HELLO, ADVENTURE SEEKER!

Life is a journey we take every day, and this
book is your very own ticket around the world.

Inside, there are 365 travel-themed activities. That's one
for **EVERY DAY OF THE YEAR.** They'll take you to faraway
countries and spectacular sites, where you'll learn fascinating
facts about the people, places, cultures, and creatures found
all over the world. Some activities will only take a minute, while
others might take much longer. You can complete them in any
order—just pick one that appeals to you, and take off!

JUST REMEMBER:

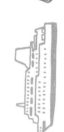

1. BE BOLD—this is a space to **EXPLORE** new ideas
    as well as places. Let your imagination run riot!

2. Know that there are **NO** wrong answers or bad ideas.

3. Have fun! **ENJOY** discovering new experiences
    with every page.

4. Once you're done, you'll have a **ONE-OF-A-KIND**
    record of your year.

BEFORE YOU GET STARTED ...

Unlike most travels and trips, you won't need much on your journey; just a pen, pencil, and some crayons or markers are enough. But here are some other useful tools that you might like to use, too:

· A globe or atlas to help you find the places mentioned and discover new ones.

· A dictionary to help you check the exact spelling and meaning of words.

OFF THE PAGE

If you're worried about changing your mind, or if you want more space to write or draw, you can use another piece of paper and stick it into the book.

DON'T STRESS

Remember, it doesn't matter if you struggle to spell, color, or draw. This book is not about grades or getting things perfect—it's your journey around the world, so have fun with it!

GO OFF-ROAD

This book is full of fascinating facts about amazing places—if something interests you, why not read more about it in other books?

1. CONGRATULATIONS! YOU'VE WON TWO TICKETS FOR YOUR DREAM VACATION. WRITE WHERE IN THE WORLD YOU'RE GOING, AND WHO'S COMING WITH YOU.

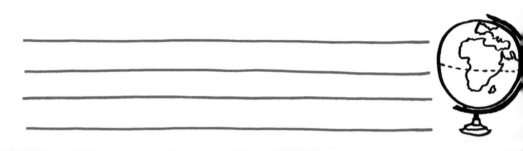

2. EVERY YEAR IN VENICE, ITALY, PEOPLE COME TOGETHER TO CELEBRATE VENICE CARNIVAL. ATTENDEES WEAR FABULOUS COSTUMES AND ELABORATE VENETIAN MASKS. DECORATE YOUR OWN VENETIAN MASK BELOW.

3. THINK OF A FAMOUS LANDMARK, SUCH AS THE EIFFEL TOWER, OR THE STATUE OF LIBERTY. DRAW II HERE—BUT GIVE IT A TWIST. YOU COULD ADD A DETAIL OR USE UNEXPECTED COLORS—GO WILD!

4. THE US DOESN'T HAVE AN OFFICIAL NATIONAL DISH, BUT MANY PEOPLE THINK OF HAMBURGERS AND APPLE PIE AS DISTINCTLY AMERICAN. IF YOU COULD CHOOSE A NEW NATIONAL DISH FOR YOUR COUNTRY, WHAT WOULD IT BE?

5. THERE ARE THOUSANDS OF DIFFERENT LANGUAGES SPOKEN AROUND THE WORLD. INVENT A NEW ONE! FIRST WRITE THE NAME OF YOUR LANGUAGE, THEN WRITE HOW TO SAY "HELLO."

6. WHERE IS THIS PLANE FLYING TO? WRITE OR DRAW YOUR ANSWER HERE.

7. EVERY COUNTRY HAS A FLAG. IF YOU WERE IN CHARGE, WHAT COLORS WOULD YOUR COUNTRY'S FLAG BE? YOU COULD COPY A REAL FLAG OR MAKE UP YOUR OWN DESIGN.

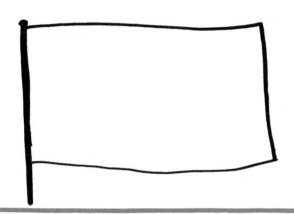

8. HAVE YOU EVER BEEN TO AN ICE HOTEL? THESE ARE REAL HOTELS MADE OF ICE AND SNOW THAT ARE BUILT EVERY WINTER FOR VISITORS TO STAY IN. DESIGN AN ICE HOTEL BELOW: WILL IT BE A SNUG IGLOO, OR A MAGNIFICENT ICE CASTLE?

9. INVENT YOUR OWN CURRENCY (MONEY), AND DESIGN THE COINS AND BANKNOTES. THEY COULD SHOW PICTURES OF PEOPLE WHO INSPIRE YOU, ANIMALS YOU LIKE, OR SIMPLE PATTERNS.

10. EVERY JANUARY 14TH IN GUJARAT, INDIA, PEOPLE GATHER FOR THE INTERNATIONAL KITE FESTIVAL. THE SKY IS FILLED WITH HUNDREDS OF COLORFUL KITES. DESIGN SOME KITES BELOW—MAKE EACH ONE UNIQUE.

11.

MANY COUNTRIES HAVE A NATIONAL MOTTO. FOR EXAMPLE, THE NATIONAL MOTTO OF KENYA IS "HARAMBEE," WHICH MEANS "ALL PULL TOGETHER." WRITE YOUR OWN NATIONAL MOTTO HERE.

- - - - - - - - - -

- - - - - - - - - -

- - - - - - - - - -

- - - - - - - - -

- - - - - - - - -

12.

PIÑATAS ARE TRADITIONAL AT LATIN AMERICAN CELEBRATIONS. THEY ARE BROKEN OPEN TO REVEAL CANDY AND TOYS INSIDE. DRAW A PIÑATA HERE. YOU COULD ADD SOMETHING UNEXPECTED FALLING OUT OF IT!

13.

MANNERS ARE DIFFERENT DEPENDING ON THE COUNTRY YOU'RE IN. FOR EXAMPLE, IN SOME PARTS OF ASIA IT'S POLITE TO BELCH AFTER EATING. USE YOUR IMAGINATION TO COMPLETE THESE SENTENCES—THE SILLIER THE BETTER!

IT IS RUDE TO ...

IT IS POLITE TO ...

14.

THERE ARE MANY WEIRD AND WONDERFUL MUSEUMS ALL OVER THE WORLD. IN JAPAN, THERE'S A MUSEUM ALL ABOUT INSTANT NOODLES! IF YOU COULD OPEN A MUSEUM DEDICATED TO ANYTHING YOU WANTED, WHAT WOULD IT BE?

THE MUSEUM OF ...

- - - - - - - - - - - - - -

- - - - - - - - - - - - - -

15.

DID YOU KNOW THAT LOTS OF COUNTRIES HAVE A NATIONAL FLOWER OR PLANT? ROSES ARE THE NATIONAL FLOWER OF THE US. IF YOU COULD PICK A NEW FLOWER, WHAT WOULD IT BE?

16.

YUNGAS ROAD IS A CYCLE ROUTE IN BOLIVIA. THE NARROW, STEEP PATH WINDS DOWN A MOUNTAIN, WITH NO GUARDRAILS. WOULD YOU CYCLE DOWN IT? WHY OR WHY NOT?

17.

"DIG THIS" IS A PARK IN LAS VEGAS, NEVADA, WHERE VISITORS CAN DRIVE FULL-SIZE DIGGERS AND OTHER CONSTRUCTION MACHINES. WHAT WOULD YOU LIKE TO DRIVE OR DO AT A DIGGER PARK?

18. DIFFERENT COUNTRIES HAVE DIFFERENT LAWS, AND SOME MIGHT SEEM A LITTLE SURPRISING. IN SINGAPORE, IT'S ILLEGAL TO SELL CHEWING GUM, AND IN THE UK, IT'S AGAINST THE LAW TO WEAR A SUIT OF ARMOR IN THE HOUSES OF PARLIAMENT. MAKE UP A LAW OF YOUR OWN!

19. THE PYRAMIDS OF GIZA IN EGYPT ARE SOME OF THE MOST VISITED TOURIST ATTRACTIONS IN THE WORLD. DRAW A SELFIE OF YOURSELF IN FRONT OF THEM!

20. SOME TRAIN JOURNEYS ARE SO LONG THAT PASSENGERS MUST SLEEP ON BOARD, IN CARRIAGES WITH BEDS. DO YOU THINK THAT WOULD BE FUN? WHY OR WHY NOT?

21. HAVE YOU HEARD OF CAT ISLAND? THIS JAPANESE ISLAND IS REALLY CALLED AOSHIMA. IT GOT ITS NICKNAME BECAUSE IT IS HOME TO MORE CATS THAN HUMANS! IMAGINE THAT YOU WASH UP ON THIS ISLAND. WHAT HAPPENS NEXT?

_____

_____

_____

_____

_____

_____

_____

_____

_____

_____

_____

_____

_____

_____

_____

22. MANY COUNTRIES HAVE A NATIONAL ANIMAL: NEW ZEALAND'S IS THE KIWI, INDONESIA CHOSE THE KOMODO DRAGON, AND SCOTLAND'S IS THE UNICORN! WHICH ANIMAL WOULD YOU CHOOSE? DRAW IT BELOW.

23. HAVE YOU EVER SEEN A CAVE PAINTING? IN PARTS OF FRANCE, THERE ARE CAVES COVERED WITH INCREDIBLE PAINTINGS OF PEOPLE AND ANIMALS. THE PAINTINGS WERE MADE ABOUT 20,000 YEARS AGO! THEY SHOW US WHAT LIFE WAS LIKE BACK THEN. DRAW ON THIS CAVE WALL. SHOW THINGS THAT REFLECT YOUR LIFE TODAY.

24. YOU'RE JETTING OFF ON A TRIP TO SOMEWHERE NEW AND EXCITING. WHAT WILL YOU PACK IN YOUR SUITCASE? WRITE YOUR DESTINATION, THEN DRAW THE ITEMS YOU'LL TAKE.

25. IF YOU WERE TO WALK ON ELAFONISI BEACH, ON THE GREEK ISLAND OF CRETE, YOU WOULD FIND PINK SAND BETWEEN YOUR TOES! GIVE THIS BEACH SAND THAT'S AN UNUSUAL COLOR.

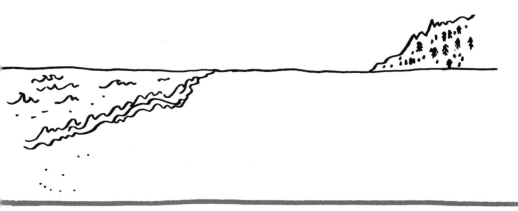

26. IN BRAZIL, SOME CHILDREN GO TO SCHOOL AT 7:00 A.M. AND FINISH AT NOON. THEY HAVE ALL AFTERNOON OFF! HOW WOULD YOU LIKE YOUR SCHOOL DAY TO BE? DESCRIBE IT HERE.

27.

WHICH FIVE COUNTRIES WOULD YOU MOST LIKE TO VISIT? PUT THEM IN ORDER, WITH YOUR FAVORITE FIRST.

1. _ _ _ _ _ _ _ _ _ _

2. _ _ _ _ _ _ _ _ _

3. _ _ _ _ _ _ _ _ _ _

4. _ _ _ _ _ _ _ _ _

5. _ _ _ _ _ _ _ _ _ _

28.

YOU'RE IN A CABLE CAR LOOKING DOWN—WHAT DO YOU SEE BELOW? WHERE IN THE WORLD ARE YOU?

29.

DIFFERENT CULTURES HAVE DIFFERENT GREETINGS. IN MANY COUNTRIES PEOPLE SHAKE HANDS OR BOW. IN NEW ZEALAND, MAORI PEOPLE RUB NOSES TO WELCOME VISITORS—THIS GREETING IS CALLED A "HONGI." AND IN ZAMBIA, YOU MIGHT SAY HELLO BY GENTLY SQUEEZING SOMEONE'S THUMB. INVENT A NEW WAY OF GREETING SOMEONE.

30.

THE VENICE ART WALLS ARE A FAMOUS LANDMARK IN VENICE BEACH,
CALIFORNIA. THE WALLS ARE COVERED IN COLORFUL GRAFFITI ART,
AND VISITORS ARE ALLOWED TO ADD THEIR OWN PAINTINGS!
DRAW WHAT YOU WOULD PAINT HERE.

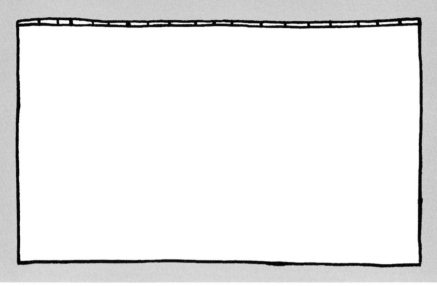

31.

EVERY YEAR NEAR GLOUCESTER, IN ENGLAND, PEOPLE GATHER TO PARTICIPATE IN
A STRANGE RACE—A CHEESE CHASE! RACERS LINE UP ON COOPER'S HILL AND RACE
DOWN THE HILL AFTER A WHEEL OF CHEESE. THE FIRST TO THE BOTTOM WINS THE
CHEESE. IMAGINE YOU'RE RUNNING IN THE RACE—WHAT HAPPENS?

32.

EVERY YEAR ON MAY 5TH, JAPAN CELEBRATES CHILDREN'S DAY. ON THIS NATIONAL HOLIDAY, FAMILIES GIVE THANKS FOR THEIR CHILDREN AND OFTEN FLY COLORFUL CARP-SHAPED WIND SOCKS, CALLED "KOINOBORI," OUTSIDE THEIR HOMES. THE FISH REPRESENT STRENGTH AND COURAGE. DESIGN YOUR OWN KOINOBORI HERE.

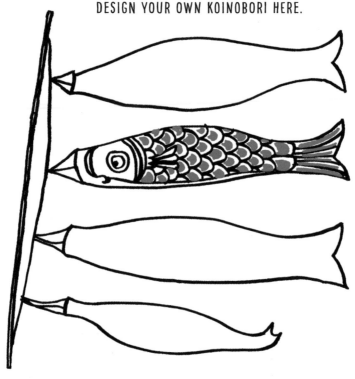

33.

CLOSE YOUR EYES AND PICTURE YOUR FAVORITE PLACE IN THE WORLD. USE THREE WORDS TO DESCRIBE IT BELOW.

34.

DO YOU KNOW WHICH COUNTRY HAS THE MOST TREES IN THE WORLD?
IT'S RUSSIA! RARE SIBERIAN TIGERS SLINK WITHIN THE DENSE FORESTS.
DRAW SOME MORE TREES FOR THIS SIBERIAN TIGER TO HIDE IN.

35.

STONEHENGE IS A CIRCLE OF STANDING STONES IN WILTSHIRE, ENGLAND,
BUILT ABOUT 5,000 YEARS AGO. THE TALLEST STONE IS OVER 28 FEET TALL.
CARHENGE IN NEBRASKA IS A REPLICA OF STONEHENGE MADE UP OF ... CARS!
INVENT YOUR OWN REPLICA MADE UP OF WHATEVER YOU LIKE.

36.

THINK OF A COUNTRY YOU'D LOVE TO VISIT, THEN DESIGN THIS POSTAGE STAMP TO REPRESENT THAT COUNTRY. YOU COULD WRITE THE NAME OR DRAW A FAMOUS LANDMARK OR PERSON FROM THERE.

37.

THE RAINIEST PLACE ON EARTH IS A VILLAGE IN INDIA CALLED MAWSYNRAM. IT GETS ABOUT 40 FEET OF RAINFALL EACH YEAR. DESIGN AN UMBRELLA FOR YOUR TRIP TO MAWSYNRAM.

38.

WHAT'S SPECIAL ABOUT JULY 7TH? IT'S WORLD CHOCOLATE DAY! IF YOU COULD PICK A FOOD FOR THE WHOLE WORLD TO CELEBRATE FOR ONE DAY, WHICH FOOD WOULD IT BE, AND WHAT DATE WOULD YOU PICK?

39.

BEFORE PAPER MONEY, DIFFERENT CULTURES AROUND THE WORLD USED DIFFERENT OBJECTS AS MONEY, INCLUDING SEASHELLS. WHAT WOULD YOU CHOOSE TO USE AS MONEY IF YOU WERE IN CHARGE?

40.

THE PYRAMIDS IN EGYPT WERE ONCE USED TO BURY IMPORTANT PEOPLE WHO
HAD DIED. THEY WERE OFTEN BUILT WITH TWISTING, NARROW PASSAGES
INSIDE TO PREVENT PEOPLE FROM STEALING TREASURE FROM THE TOMBS.
DESIGN A MAZE FOR THIS PYRAMID TO CONFUSE ROBBERS.

41. THE GOBI DESERT IN MONGOLIA IS A LONG WAY FROM ANY CITIES, SO THE SKY IS VERY DARK AT NIGHT—PERFECT FOR STARGAZING. DRAW LOTS OF STARS AND PLANETS IN THIS PICTURE OF THE SKY OVER THE GOBI.

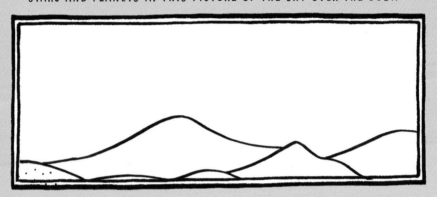

42. THERE ARE SOME UNUSUAL SPORTS AROUND THE WORLD, INCLUDING LAWNMOWER RACING, TOE WRESTLING, AND EXTREME IRONING—WHERE PEOPLE IRON WHILE SKYDIVING, OR UNDERWATER! INVENT THREE NEW OFFBEAT SPORTS.

1. _____

2. _____

3. _____

43. SOME TYPES OF HAT ARE SEEN AS SYMBOLS OF CERTAIN COUNTRIES. THE SOMBRERO IS OFTEN ASSOCIATED WITH MEXICO, FOR EXAMPLE, WHILE THE BERET IS A SYMBOL OF FRANCE. DESIGN A NEW HAT THAT REPRESENTS YOUR COUNTRY.

44. ARTIFICIAL ISLANDS ARE MADE BY DROPPING SAND OR SOIL INTO THE OCEAN. DURRAT AL BAHRAIN IS A GROUP OF ARTIFICIAL ISLANDS OFF THE COAST OF BAHRAIN. SOME OF THE ISLANDS ARE SHAPED LIKE FISH! WHAT SHAPE WOULD YOU CHOOSE FOR AN ARTIFICIAL ISLAND? DRAW IT HERE.

45. THE COLOSSEUM IN ROME, ITALY, WAS A KIND OF THEATER, USED 2,000 YEARS AGO FOR STAGING BATTLES BETWEEN PEOPLE AND ANIMALS. IMAGINE YOU TIME TRAVEL TO ANCIENT ROME AND END UP IN THE MIDDLE OF THE COLOSSEUM! DESCRIBE WHAT HAPPENS.

46.

HAVE YOU HEARD OF THE LOCH NESS MONSTER? THIS LEGENDARY CREATURE IS SAID TO LIVE IN A LAKE IN SCOTLAND—SOME PEOPLE BELIEVE IT'S REAL, WHILE OTHERS THINK IT'S A HOAX. MAKE UP A MONSTER LEGEND FOR WHERE YOU LIVE.

DESCRIBE WHAT IT LOOKS LIKE, WHERE IT LIVES, AND WHAT IT DOES.

_____

_____

_____

_____

_____

_____

_____

47.

IMAGINE YOU'RE THE FIRST TO FLY AN AIRPLANE AROUND THE WORLD. WRITE ABOUT HOW YOU FEEL WHEN YOU FINISH YOUR JOURNEY.

_____

_____

_____

_____

_____

_____

_____

48.

IN PARTS OF SOUTH AMERICA, YOU CAN FIND ROPE BRIDGES HIGH UP OVER GORGES AND RIVERS. MANY WERE BUILT IN THE 1400S TO CONNECT PARTS OF THE INCA EMPIRE. DRAW A SWAYING ROPE BRIDGE BETWEEN THESE CLIFFS.

49.

MANY CITIES AROUND THE WORLD HAVE STATUES OF FAMOUS PEOPLE WHO LIVED OR WERE BORN THERE. IN KINGSTON, JAMAICA, FOR EXAMPLE, THERE IS A STATUE OF REGGAE STAR BOB MARLEY. DRAW A STATUE OF YOURSELF FOR YOUR HOMETOWN!

50.

THE LEANING TOWER OF PISA IN ITALY IS FAMOUS FOR THE WAY IT LEANS AT AN ANGLE. INVENT A FUNNY REASON FOR WHY IT LEANS.

51. MOUNT EVEREST IN THE HIMALAYAS IS THE HIGHEST MOUNTAIN ON EARTH (ABOVE SEA LEVEL). IT'S 29,032 FEET TALL. IMAGINE YOU'RE CLIMBING TO THE PEAK—WRITE ABOUT YOUR EXPEDITION. ARE YOU ALONE? IS THERE A BLIZZARD? WHAT HAPPENS WHEN YOU MAKE IT TO THE TOP?

_____

_____

_____

_____

_____

_____

_____

_____

_____

52. SOME COUNTRIES HAVE A NATIONAL SPORT. IN SRI LANKA, IT'S VOLLEYBALL. IF YOU COULD CHOOSE YOUR COUNTRY'S NATIONAL SPORT, WHAT WOULD IT BE?

53. THE DEAD SEA IS ACTUALLY A LAKE IN SOUTHWESTERN ASIA. ITS WATERS ARE SO SALTY THAT NO PLANTS OR ANIMALS CAN LIVE THERE. ALL THAT SALT ALSO MAKES IT EASIER TO FLOAT! WRITE A STORY ABOUT SOMETHING UNEXPECTED FLOATING ON THE SURFACE OF THE LAKE.

_____

_____

_____

_____

_____

_____

54. ALL OVER THE WORLD THERE ARE DIFFERENT KINDS OF HOMES, INCLUDING SKY-HIGH APARTMENTS, HOUSEBOATS, SINGLE-STORY BUNGALOWS, CABINS, HOMES ON STILTS, COTTAGES, AND MORE! WHAT WOULD BE YOUR PERFECT HOME? DRAW IT HERE.

55.

THE WORLD'S TALLEST BUILDING IS THE BURJ KHALIFA. IT'S IN DUBAI AND MEASURES A HUGE 2,722 FEET TALL. DESIGN AN EVEN TALLER BUILDING NEXT TO IT!

56.

AT AIRPORTS AROUND THE WORLD, SIGNS WELCOME VISITORS TO CITIES AND COUNTRIES. WRITE A MESSAGE TO GO IN YOUR CLOSEST AIRPORT, WELCOMING PEOPLE TO THE AREA.

_____

_____

_____

_____

_____

_____

_____

57.

DESIGN A BOAT OR RAFT BELOW. WHERE IN THE WORLD WOULD YOU SAIL IT TO?

58.

YOU'RE ON A HELICOPTER RIDE WITH YOUR BEST FRIEND. WHERE ARE YOU, AND WHAT CAN YOU SEE?

59.

HAVE YOU HEARD OF A YETI? LEGEND SAYS THESE HUGE, FURRY CREATURES LIVE IN THE SNOWY MOUNTAINS OF THE HIMALAYAS. SOME PEOPLE CLAIM TO HAVE SEEN THEM, BUT MOST BELIEVE THEY AREN'T REAL. DRAW A YETI'S FOOTPRINT BELOW.

60.

THERE ARE MANY BEAUTIFUL ANCIENT ROMAN MOSAICS TO SEE IN ITALY. MOSAICS ARE PICTURES MADE FROM TINY PIECES OF COLORED TILE. MAKE A MOSAIC OF YOUR OWN BY COLORING THESE TILES ANY WAY YOU LIKE.

61.

MARCH IS BEOT-KKOT, OR CHERRY BLOSSOM, SEASON IN SOUTH KOREA.
PEOPLE TRAVEL FROM ALL OVER TO SEE THESE PINK TREES IN FULL BLOOM.
ADD SOME PINK CHERRY BLOSSOMS TO THESE TREES.

62.

AT A FESTIVAL CALLED "LA TOMATINA" IN BUÑOL, SPAIN, PEOPLE THROW RIPE TOMATOES AT EACH OTHER. MAKE UP A FUNNY FESTIVAL OF YOUR OWN. WHAT IS IT CALLED? WHAT HAPPENS THERE?

63.

HAVE YOU NOTICED THAT ITALY IS SHAPED LIKE A LONG BOOT WITH A HIGH HEEL? INVENT A FUNNY-SHAPED COUNTRY AND DRAW IT HERE. WHAT IS IT CALLED?

64.

MAKE UP A SILLY STORY ABOUT A PLANE RIDE. PERHAPS THE PILOT IS A PENGUIN,
OR MAYBE YOUR FAVORITE POP STAR IS SITTING NEXT TO YOU—IT'S UP TO YOU!

_____

_____

_____

_____

_____

_____

_____

_____

_____

_____

_____

_____

_____

_____

_____

65.

THINK OF PAST VACATIONS, TRAVELS, OR ADVENTURES YOU'VE BEEN ON, OR IMAGINE SOME, THEN FILL THE PHOTO FRAMES WITH DRAWINGS OF THOSE MEMORIES OR IDEAS.

66.

AT THE BOTTOM OF THE MEDITERRANEAN SEA, THERE ARE MANY OLD SHIPWRECKS. DIVERS EXPLORE THEM AND SOMETIMES BRING BACK OBJECTS. IMAGINE THAT YOU'RE EXPLORING A WRECK, AND YOU FIND A SPECIAL OBJECT. WHAT IS IT?

67.

IF YOU COULD GO ON A SAFARI IN KENYA, WHICH AFRICAN ANIMALS WOULD YOU BE MOST EXCITED TO SEE? LIST THEM HERE.

68.

HAVE YOU EVER BEEN ON A ZIP LINE? THERE'S A ZIP LINE IN SPAIN WHICH LETS YOU GO BACK IN TIME! IT STARTS IN SPAIN AND FINISHES IN PORTUGAL—WHICH IS 1 HOUR BEHIND. DRAW YOURSELF RIDING THE ZIP LINE BELOW.

69.

THE EQUATOR IS AN IMAGINARY LINE AROUND THE MIDDLE OF OUR PLANET. PLACES NEAR THE EQUATOR ARE HOT AND HUMID, WHILE COUNTRIES FARTHER FROM THE EQUATOR HAVE SEASONS OF HOT AND COLD WEATHER. WHERE WOULD YOU RATHER LIVE?

70.

DURING THE DRAGON BOAT FESTIVAL IN CHINA, PEOPLE RACE LONG ROWBOATS WITH A DRAGON'S HEAD AND TAIL AT THE ENDS. DESIGN YOUR OWN DRAGON BOAT.

71.

ON OCTOBER 31ST, MANY PEOPLE AROUND THE WORLD CELEBRATE HALLOWEEN. CHILDREN OFTEN DRESS IN COSTUMES AND GO TRICK-OR-TREATING. DESIGN YOUR OWN HALLOWEEN COSTUME.

72.

MORE THAN THREE MILLION BATS LIVE IN THE DEVIL'S SINKHOLE IN TEXAS. IT'S A VERTICAL CAVE 400 FEET DEEP. ON SUMMER EVENINGS, THEY ALL FLY OUT IN A SWIRLING SWARM. LIST FIVE WORDS YOU MIGHT USE TO DESCRIBE THEM.

1. _____

2. _____

3. _____

4. _____

5. _____

73.

LAKE KLILUK IN CANADA IS A COLLECTION OF GIANT PUDDLES! A LOCAL BELIEF
IS THAT EACH OF ITS 365 POOLS HAS ITS OWN UNIQUE HEALING POWER.
IN EACH PUDDLE BELOW, WRITE WHAT YOU THINK ITS POWER WOULD BE.

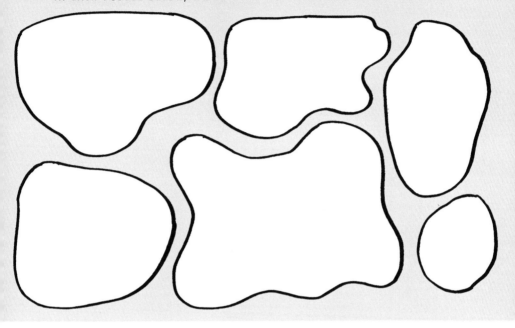

74.

LAS FALLAS DE VALÈNCIA IS A SPANISH FESTIVAL DURING WHICH PEOPLE
PARADE HUGE STATUES AROUND THE CITY OF VALÈNCIA, THEN BURN THEM.
SOME SAY IT STARTED WITH CARPENTERS USING UP SPARE WOOD ON THE
DAY BEFORE THE FEAST OF ST. JOSEPH, THEIR PATRON SAINT. WHAT WOULD
YOU MAKE A MODEL OF? HOW WOULD YOU FEEL ABOUT BURNING IT?

75.

A MIRAGE IS AN IMAGE OF SOMETHING THAT ISN'T THERE. IN DESERTS, PEOPLE SOMETIMES SEE MIRAGES OF CITIES OR FORESTS. DRAW A MIRAGE IN THIS DESERT.

76.

MUSIC FESTIVALS TAKE PLACE IN UNUSUAL LOCATIONS AROUND THE WORLD, FROM INSIDE GLACIERS IN ICELAND TO THE SEABED OFF THE COAST OF FLORIDA—YES, REALLY! FILL IN THIS POSTER WITH THE DETAILS OF YOUR OWN MADE-UP FESTIVAL.

- WHERE IS IT HELD?
- WHO'S PLAYING?
- WHAT CAN PEOPLE DO THERE?

77.

SOME TEA IS MADE FROM THE LEAVES OF TEA BUSHES THAT GROW IN INDIA AND CHINA. PEOPLE IN THESE COUNTRIES DRINK A LOT OF TEA. DECORATE A LOVELY TEAPOT TO BREW IT IN!

78.

ALL OVER THE WORLD YOU CAN FIND INTERESTING SCULPTURES. IN LIÈGE, BELGIUM, THERE IS A CLOTHESPIN THAT HOLDS UP A FOLD OF THE GRASS-COVERED GROUND. INVENT AN UNUSUAL SCULPTURE IN THIS SPACE.

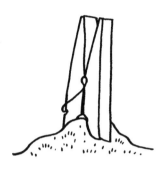

79.

THE LONGEST RIVER IN THE WORLD IS THE NILE. IT STARTS IN CENTRAL AFRICA AND RUNS NORTH TO THE MEDITERRANEAN SEA, OVER 4,100 MILES. IMAGINE YOU TOOK A JOURNEY ALONG IT. WRITE A LOG OF HOW YOU TRAVELED AND WHAT IT WAS LIKE.

80.

IN MANY PARTS OF THE WORLD, PEOPLE CELEBRATE CHRISTMAS BY PUTTING UP A FIR TREE IN THEIR HOMES AND DECORATING IT WITH LIGHTS AND ORNAMENTS. DRAW A DIFFERENT KIND OF TREE IN THE SPACE BELOW AND DECORATE IT HOWEVER YOU LIKE.

81.

THE WORLD'S LONGEST TOBOGGAN RUN IS CALLED BIG PINTENFRITZ. IT RUNS FOR 9 MILES DOWN THE JUNGFRAU MOUNTAIN IN THE ALPS. WHAT DO YOU THINK IT WOULD BE LIKE TO TOBOGGAN DOWN IT?

82.

THE LONGEST MOUNTAIN RANGE IN THE WORLD IS THE MID-OCEAN RIDGE. IT'S ALMOST ENTIRELY UNDERWATER! WHAT DO YOU THINK YOU MIGHT SEE ON THESE UNDERSEA MOUNTAINS? DRAW IT HERE.

83.

A TRADITION AMONG THE NANAI PEOPLE OF RUSSIA AND CHINA IS TO MAKE CLOTHES OUT OF FISH SKIN. DESIGN YOUR OWN OUTFIT MADE FROM SCALY FISH SKIN.

84.

THERE ARE NO CARS ALLOWED ON SARK, A TINY ISLAND OFF THE COAST OF FRANCE. PEOPLE USE BICYCLES, HORSE-DRAWN CARTS, AND EVEN TRACTORS TO GET AROUND. DRAW THE MODE OF TRANSPORT YOU WOULD USE TO TRAVEL AROUND SARK.

85.

THE UNDERGROUND CAVE OF CRYSTALS IN CHIHUAHUA, MEXICO, IS FAMOUS FOR THE HUGE CRYSTALS THAT HAVE FORMED INSIDE IT. THE LARGEST IS 37 FEET LONG. FILL THIS CAVE WITH CRYSTALS.

86.

ANTARCTICA IS SO COLD THAT IT HAS NO LARGE LAND ANIMALS. BUT IMAGINE THAT YOU DISCOVER THE FIRST ONE! WHAT IS IT LIKE? DESCRIBE OR DRAW IT HERE.

87.

THERE'S A STATION ON THE LONDON UNDERGROUND CALLED "ELEPHANT AND CASTLE." DRAW THE FIRST THING THIS NAME MAKES YOU THINK OF.

88.

MANY CITIES AND TOWNS HAVE A SQUARE WHERE PEOPLE CAN HOLD CELEBRATIONS, MARKETS, AND OTHER EVENTS. THINK UP A SQUARE FOR WHERE YOU LIVE. WHAT WILL IT BE CALLED? WHAT EVENTS WILL HAPPEN THERE?

89.

THERE ARE LOTS OF DIFFERENT ROAD SIGNS AROUND THE WORLD. THIS ONE, FROM GREENLAND, MEANS "LOOK OUT FOR SLEDS CROSSING THE ROAD." MAKE UP TWO NEW ROAD SIGNS OF YOUR OWN.

90. IN SCOTLAND, A TRADITIONAL MUSICAL INSTRUMENT IS THE BAGPIPE. IT HAS A LARGE BAG WHICH CONTAINS AIR, AND PIPES THAT MAKE A SOUND WHEN THE AIR IS SQUEEZED THROUGH THEM. INVENT AN UNUSUAL MUSICAL INSTRUMENT OF YOUR OWN. DRAW OR DESCRIBE IT HERE.

91. THE BUDDHIST TEMPLE ANGKOR WAT IN CAMBODIA IS SURROUNDED BY A 650-FOOT-WIDE MOAT— A WATER-FILLED TRENCH DUG TO PROTECT THE TEMPLE AND COLLECT RAINWATER. DESIGN YOUR OWN MOAT BELOW.

92. IN CAPPADOCIA, TURKEY, SOME PEOPLE LIVE IN HOMES MADE IN CAVES, A TRADITION THAT STRETCHES BACK HUNDREDS OF YEARS. WRITE AN AD TO ENCOURAGE PEOPLE TO COME AND STAY IN A CAVE HOME.

93. THE ALHAMBRA IS A PALACE AND FORTRESS IN SPAIN THAT IS OVER 1,100 YEARS OLD. IT'S FAMOUS FOR ITS BEAUTIFUL DECORATED TILES. CONTINUE THIS PATTERN OF TILES TO FILL THE BOX, THEN COLOR IT IN.

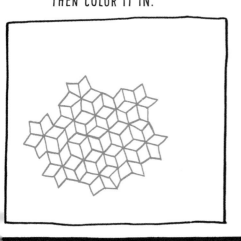

94. THE LARGEST STADIUM EVER BUILT WAS THE GREAT STRAHOV STADIUM IN PRAGUE, CZECH REPUBLIC. IT COULD HOLD 220,000 PEOPLE. WHICH THREE SPORTS OR EVENTS WOULD YOU MOST LIKE TO SEE IN A HUGE STADIUM?

1. _____

2. _____

3. _____

95. IN UFFINGTON, ENGLAND, IN THE BRONZE AGE, A GIGANTIC WHITE HORSE WAS CARVED IN THE CHALKY HILLSIDE, AND IS STILL THERE TODAY. NO ONE KNOWS FOR SURE WHY IT WAS CARVED. IF THERE WAS A CHALKY HILL NEAR WHERE YOU LIVE, WHAT GIANT PICTURE WOULD YOU CUT INTO IT, AND WHY?

96.

MANY ISLANDS IN THE MEDITERRANEAN SEA HAVE SANDY BEACHES, AND IN THE SUMMER THE SEA IS OFTEN WARM AND CALM. WHAT WOULD YOU LIKE TO DO ON A VISIT TO A MEDITERRANEAN BEACH?

97.

ST. BASIL'S CATHEDRAL IS AN AMAZING CHURCH IN MOSCOW, RUSSIA, WITH LOTS OF TOWERS TOPPED WITH DECORATED, ONION-SHAPED DOMES. COLOR IN THE CATHEDRAL AND ADD MORE TOWERS AND DOMES!

98.

AT THE LOPBURI MONKEY BUFFET FESTIVAL IN THAILAND, THE LOCAL MONKEYS ARE HONORED WITH A SPECTACULAR FEAST. FILL THIS TABLE WITH DELICIOUS FRUITS AND VEGETABLES FOR THESE LONG-TAILED MACAQUES TO ENJOY.

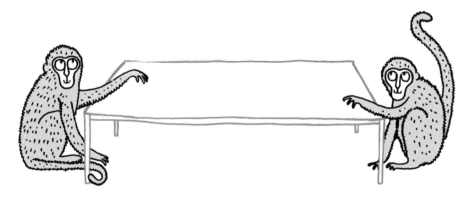

99.

THE INTERNATIONAL DATE LINE RUNS FROM THE NORTH POLE TO THE SOUTH POLE. YOU CAN STAND WITH ONE FOOT IN TODAY AND THE OTHER IN TOMORROW! WRITE A STORY ABOUT BEING ABLE TO JUMP BETWEEN TWO DAYS.

_____

_____

_____

_____

_____

_____

_____

_____

100.

IN CHERRAPUNJI, INDIA, LOCALS GROW THE ROOTS OF TREES ACROSS RIVERS TO MAKE STURDY, NATURAL BRIDGES. DRAW A TANGLED, JUNGLE TREE-ROOT BRIDGE CONNECTING THESE TREES OVER A RIVER.

101.

HALF DOME IS A HIGH CLIFF IN YOSEMITE NATIONAL PARK, IN CALIFORNIA. CLIMBERS USE A STEEP CABLE LADDER TO REACH THE TOP FOR SPECTACULAR VIEWS. LIST THREE WORDS TO DESCRIBE YOUR FEELINGS IF YOU REACHED THE TOP.

1. _____

2. _____

3. _____

102.

IN CHINA, EACH YEAR IS ASSIGNED TO AN ANIMAL IN THE CHINESE ZODIAC: RAT, OX, TIGER, RABBIT, DRAGON, SNAKE, HORSE, GOAT, MONKEY, ROOSTER, DOG, AND PIG. MAKE UP YOUR OWN ZODIAC OF 12 ANIMALS. CIRCLE THE ONE WHOSE YEAR YOU WOULD LIKE TO HAVE BEEN BORN IN.

1. _____
2. _____
3. _____
4. _____
5. _____
6. _____
7. _____
8. _____
9. _____
10. _____
11. _____
12. _____

103.

JUST OFF THE COAST OF ALEXANDRIA BAY, NEW YORK, IS THE WORLD'S SMALLEST INHABITED ISLAND. IT HAS ONE HOUSE ON IT! DRAW THE HOUSE YOU WOULD BUILD IF YOU HAD A TINY ISLAND.

104.

IN 2014, A GERMAN FISHERMAN DISCOVERED A POSTCARD IN A GLASS BOTTLE FLOATING IN THE BALTIC SEA. IT WAS 101 YEARS OLD! WHAT WOULD YOU WRITE ON A POSTCARD FOR SOMEONE A CENTURY LATER?

105.

PEOPLE OFTEN TRAVEL ABROAD TO SEE ANIMALS SUCH AS TIGERS, ELEPHANTS, OR KOALAS IN THEIR NATURAL HABITAT. WHICH THREE ANIMALS WOULD YOU MOST LIKE TO SEE IN THE WILD? WHERE WOULD YOU GO TO SEE THEM?

1.

2.

3.

_____   _____   _____

_____   _____   _____

106.

IN THE ALPS MOUNTAINS IN EUROPE, TRAINS AND CARS OFTEN TRAVEL THROUGH LONG, DARK TUNNELS. WHAT DO YOU THINK IT'S LIKE TO GO THROUGH A LONG TUNNEL CUT INTO THE SOLID ROCK OF A MOUNTAIN?

107. THE MEDITERRANEAN ISLAND OF MADEIRA HAS A YEARLY FLOWER FESTIVAL WITH A PARADE OF FLOATS COVERED IN FLOWERS. DESIGN YOUR OWN FLOWER-COVERED FLOAT FOR THE PARADE.

108. KICK-'EM-JENNY IS AN UNDERWATER VOLCANO IN THE CARIBBEAN SEA. FINISH THIS DRAWING TO SHOW WHAT IT MIGHT LOOK LIKE ERUPTING UNDERWATER.

109. SMILEY FACE FOREST IN WILLAMINA, OREGON, WAS MADE BY PLANTING DIFFERENT KINDS OF TREES IN A PATTERN. THE FIR TREES STAY GREEN, BUT THE LARCH TREES TURN YELLOW IN THE FALL, MAKING A SMILEY DESIGN. COLOR THESE TREES SO THAT THE FOREST LOOKS LIKE A FACE.

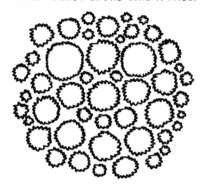

110. THE DEEPEST POINT ON EARTH IS CHALLENGER DEEP, AT THE BOTTOM OF THE PACIFIC OCEAN. ONLY A HANDFUL OF PEOPLE HAVE EVER BEEN THERE, IN SPECIAL SUBMARINES. WOULD YOU WANT TO GO? WHY?

111. IN NICARAGUA, THERE ARE NO STREET NAMES OR ADDRESSES. INSTEAD, DIRECTIONS ARE GIVEN USING NEARBY LANDMARKS. FOR EXAMPLE: "FROM THE OLD THEATER, TWO BLOCKS NORTH, ONE BLOCK EAST." MAKE UP NICARAGUAN-STYLE DIRECTIONS TO YOUR HOME.

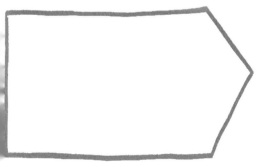

112.

GIANT'S CAUSEWAY IS A GROUP OF LARGE STONE COLUMNS ON THE COAST OF NORTHERN IRELAND. ONE LEGEND SAYS THEY WERE LEFT OVER FROM A PATH THROUGH THE SEA MADE BY GIANTS. IMAGINE YOU WERE ONE OF THE GIANTS. WHERE DID YOUR PATH LEAD?

113.

IN SUCEAVA, ROMANIA, THERE'S A HOUSE CUT OUT OF A BOULDER. IT WAS MADE MORE THAN 500 YEARS AGO BY A MONK USING ONLY A CHISEL. TURN THIS ROCK INTO A HOUSE—TRY ADDING DOORS, WINDOWS, AND CHIMNEYS.

114.

TOWER BRIDGE IN LONDON, ENGLAND, OPENS IN THE MIDDLE TO ALLOW SHIPS TO PASS THROUGH. DRAW A SHIP GOING THROUGH THE BRIDGE.

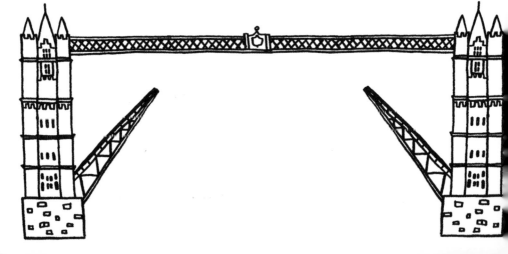

115.

THERE ARE MANY AIRLINES YOU CAN USE TO TAKE A TRIP. THEY ALL HAVE DIFFERENT DESIGNS ON THE TAILS OF THEIR PLANES—AND SOMETIMES ALL OVER THEM. IF YOU HAD AN AIRLINE, WHAT WOULD THE PLANES LOOK LIKE? DRAW OR DESCRIBE THEM.

116.

INUKSUIT ARE MONUMENTS MADE BY PILING UP STONES TO LOOK LIKE HUMAN FIGURES, CROSSES, OR COLUMNS. THEY ARE MADE BY INUIT PEOPLE IN CANADA AND GREENLAND, WHO USE SOME OF THEM A BIT LIKE SIGNPOSTS. DRAW YOUR OWN INUKSUIT HERE.

117.

AMBULUWAWA TOWER IN SRI LANKA HAS A SPIRAL STAIRCASE WINDING AROUND THE OUTSIDE OF IT. WHAT WOULD IT BE LIKE TO CLIMB IT?

118.

DURING THE GREAT PUMPKIN REGATTA IN TUALATIN, OREGON, PEOPLE RACE BOATS MADE FROM GIANT, HOLLOWED-OUT PUMPKINS. WHAT MASSIVE FRUIT OR VEGETABLE WOULD YOU MAKE A BOAT FROM, AND WHY?

119.

THE TAJ MAHAL IN INDIA IS MADE OF WHITE MARBLE. GIVE IT A MAKEOVER BELOW.

120.

THERE ARE STILL PARTS OF EARTH THAT HAVE NEVER BEEN EXPLORED, DEEP IN THE AMAZON RAIN FOREST OR THE WILDS OF SIBERIA. IMAGINE YOU'RE LEADING AN EXPEDITION TO ONE OF THESE PLACES. DESIGN AN AD ASKING FOR PEOPLE TO SIGN UP. REMEMBER TO INCLUDE WHERE YOU'LL BE GOING, WHY YOU'RE GOING THERE, AND WHAT QUALITIES GOOD EXPLORERS WILL NEED.

121. KANINHOPPNING IS THE SWEDISH SPORT OF BUNNY RACING.
RABBITS ARE LED AROUND A CIRCUIT AND JUMP OVER THINGS.
ADD JUMPS, OBSTACLES, AND A FINISH LINE TO THIS BUNNY RACE.

122. THE "RAINBOW MOUNTAINS" OF ZHANGYE, CHINA, ARE STRIPED WITH RED,
YELLOW, ORANGE, BLUE, AND GREEN MINERALS. MAKE UP A LEGEND THAT
GIVES A FANTASTICAL REASON FOR THE MOUNTAINS' UNIQUE LOOK.

123. IN SOME PARTS OF THE WORLD, PEOPLE CAN WATCH SHARKS FROM A PROTECTIVE CAGE LOWERED INTO THE WATER. IMAGINE YOU'RE A SHARK SEEING PEOPLE IN A CAGE. WHAT IS YOUR FIRST THOUGHT?

124. WHAT'S THE MOST SURPRISING THING YOU COULD FIND AT THE TOP OF MOUNT EVEREST?

125. MILLIONS OF CONTAINER SHIPS CARRYING FOOD AND OTHER GOODS TRAVEL THE WORLD EVERY DAY. WHERE DO YOU THINK THIS CONTAINER SHIP IS GOING? WHERE IS IT COMING FROM? WHAT IS IT CARRYING?

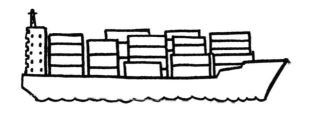

126.

YOU CAN CLIMB A SPIRAL STAIRCASE INSIDE THE STATUE OF LIBERTY IN NEW YORK AND LOOK OUT OF THE CROWN. IMAGINE IF THE STATUE COULD TALK. WHAT WOULD SHE SAY TO THE PEOPLE WALKING AROUND INSIDE HER HEAD?

127.

FIREWORKS WERE INVENTED IN CHINA AROUND 1,000 YEARS AGO. IMAGINE THAT YOU ARE ONE OF THE FIRST PEOPLE EVER TO SEE AND HEAR FIREWORKS. WHAT ARE YOUR THOUGHTS AND FEELINGS?

128.

VENICE, IN ITALY, HAS CANALS AND SIDEWALKS INSTEAD OF STREETS. PEOPLE MOVE AROUND BY BOAT OR ON FOOT. INVENT A NEW WAY OF GETTING AROUND YOUR HOMETOWN OR CITY.

129.

HOUSES ON STILTS ARE FOUND ALL OVER THE WORLD, FROM THE ARCTIC TO THE PACIFIC ISLANDS. THE STILTS PROTECT THE HOUSE FROM FLOODING, AND PESTS, LIKE RATS. DESIGN A HOUSE ON STILTS THAT YOU WOULD LIKE TO LIVE IN.

130.

THE TOMB OF THE FIRST EMPEROR OF CHINA, QIN SHI HUANG, CONTAINS AN ARMY OF STATUES THAT INCLUDES MORE THAN 8,000 LIFE-SIZE SOLDIERS, 500 HORSES, AND 100 CHARIOTS, INTENDED TO PROTECT HIM IN THE AFTERLIFE. IF YOU RULED AN EMPIRE, WHAT WOULD YOU HAVE BURIED WITH YOU? LIST OR DRAW THE ITEMS BELOW.

131.

THE TALLEST TREE IN THE WORLD IS A COAST REDWOOD IN REDWOOD NATIONAL PARK, IN CALIFORNIA. IT IS 380 FEET TALL. IMAGINE YOU COULD CLIMB IT—WHAT WOULD YOU SEE FROM THE TOP?

132.

OLD FAITHFUL IS A GEYSER—A NATURAL FOUNTAIN THAT SPURTS BOILING HOT WATER FAR INTO THE AIR. IT IS IN YELLOWSTONE NATIONAL PARK IN WYOMING. DRAW SOMETHING BENEATH THE GROUND AS A MADE-UP REASON FOR OLD FAITHFUL'S ERUPTIONS.

133.

THE EUROSTAR IS A TRAIN THAT TRAVELS THROUGH AN UNDERWATER TUNNEL BETWEEN FRANCE AND ENGLAND. IMAGINE IF THERE WAS NO TUNNEL, AND PASSENGERS COULD SEE OUT THE WINDOW INTO THE SEA. DESCRIBE THE VIEW.

134.

THE WORLD'S LARGEST CAVE IS HANG SƠN ĐOÒNG IN VIETNAM.
A PASSENGER PLANE COULD FLY THROUGH IT WITHOUT TOUCHING
THE SIDES. DRAW SOMETHING HUGE AND UNUSUAL IN THE CAVE.

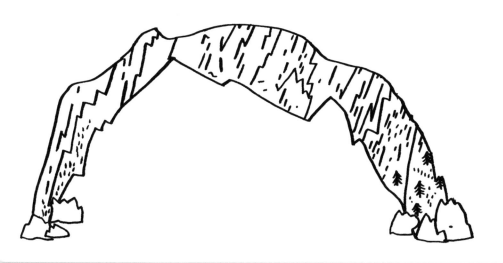

135.

SNOWBOARDING IS A POPULAR SPORT WHEREVER SNOWY SLOPES ARE TO BE
FOUND, SUCH AS FRANCE, THE US, AND CANADA. MANY SNOWBOARDS HAVE
EYE-POPPING DESIGNS. DECORATE YOUR OWN SNOWBOARD BELOW.

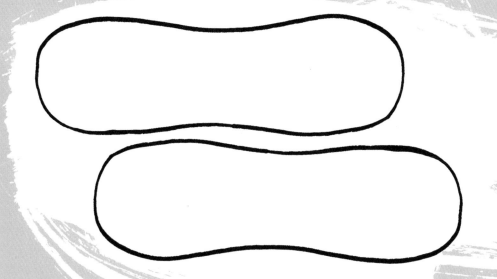

136.

IF SOMEONE WAS COMING TO VISIT YOUR COUNTRY, WHICH THREE THINGS WOULD YOU RECOMMEND THEY SEE?

1. _ _ _ _ _ _ _ _ _ _

2. _ _ _ _ _ _ _ _ _ _ _

3. _ _ _ _ _ _ _ _ _

137.

TO MANY PEOPLE IN INDIA, THE COW IS A SACRED ANIMAL. IT CANNOT BE HARMED AND MUST BE CAREFULLY LOOKED AFTER. IF YOU COULD PROTECT ONE SPECIES OF ANIMAL AND GIVE IT SPECIAL TREATMENT, WHAT WOULD IT BE?

138.

NASA LAUNCHES ASTRONAUTS INTO SPACE FROM THE COAST OF FLORIDA. WRITE A DIARY ENTRY FROM THE POINT OF VIEW OF AN ASTRONAUT LEAVING EARTH FOR THE FIRST TIME.

139.

THE CHILDREN'S RAILWAY IN BUDAPEST, HUNGARY, IS A TRAIN STAFFED ALMOST ENTIRELY BY KIDS. CHILDREN BETWEEN 10 AND 14 YEARS OLD WORK ON THE LINE: SELLING TICKETS, GIVING SIGNALS, AND DRIVING THE TRAIN. IF YOU COULD LET CHILDREN RUN ONE THING, WHAT WOULD IT BE, AND WHY?

- -

- -

- -

- -

140.

MANY CITIES AROUND THE WORLD, SUCH AS NEW YORK CITY, HAVE FAMOUS SKYLINES (THE VIEW OF THEIR BUILDINGS AND LAND AS SEEN FROM FAR AWAY). ADD SOMETHING SILLY TO THIS MADE-UP SKYLINE.

141.

THE INDIAN CITY OF JODHPUR
HAS THOUSANDS OF BLUE HOUSES,
WHICH SOME SAY HONOR THE HINDU
GOD SHIVA, WHO HAS BLUE SKIN.
WHAT COLOR WOULD YOU LIKE
HOUSES NEAR YOU TO BE?

142.

ROBOTAZIA IS A RESTAURANT
IN MILTON KEYNES, ENGLAND,
WHERE THE WAITERS ARE ROBOTS.
DESIGN YOUR OWN ROBOT
WAITER TO WORK THERE.

143.

MAPS HELP US FIND OUR WAY AROUND AN AREA. DRAW A MAP
OF YOUR LOCAL AREA, SHOWING THE ROUTE FROM YOUR HOME
TO SCHOOL, OR TO A PLACE YOU PARTICULARLY LIKE.

144.

ZHANGJIAJIE NATIONAL PARK IN CHINA HAS TOWERING COLUMNS
OF ROCK SPRINKLED WITH DENSE FORESTS. FINISH THIS VIEW OF
THE PARK BY ADDING MORE COLUMNS AND TREES.

145.

AT LONG ISLAND, IN THE BAHAMAS,
THERE'S A HOLE BENEATH THE WATER!
IT'S A SINKHOLE IN THE SEABED OVER
600 FEET DEEP. MAKE UP A CREATURE
THAT COULD LIVE AT THE BOTTOM
AND DRAW IT HERE.

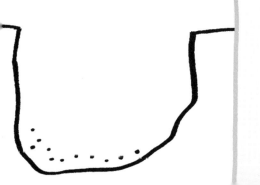

146.

DID YOU KNOW THERE'S NO ACTUAL
POLE AT THE NORTH POLE? DESIGN
A POLE THAT COULD BE USED
TO MARK THIS FAMOUS SPOT.

147. ON FEBRUARY 2ND, GROUNDHOG DAY, PEOPLE IN PUNXSUTAWNEY, PENNSYLVANIA, WATCH A GROUNDHOG NAMED PHIL PREDICT THE FUTURE! IF IT'S SUNNY, AND PHIL CAN SEE HIS SHADOW, WINTER WILL LAST ANOTHER SIX WEEKS. DRAW THE SUN AND PHIL'S SHADOW.

148. PAMUKKALE, TURKEY, HAS TERRACES OF NATURAL HOT POOLS OF MINERAL-RICH WATER. DRAW YOURSELF ENJOYING A DIP IN ONE.

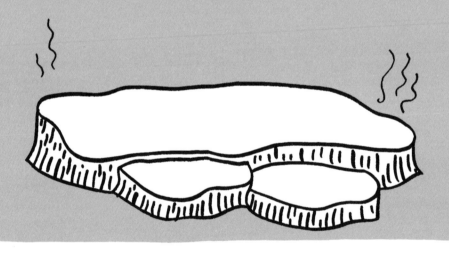

149. IN JAPAN, YOU CAN VISIT SPECIAL GARDENS, CALLED "KARESANSUI." THEY ARE ARRANGEMENTS OF STONES, GRAVEL, MOSS, AND STICKS, WITHOUT GRASS OR LEAFY PLANTS. USE THIS SPACE TO DRAW YOUR OWN GARDEN WITH NO PLANTS

150. THE OLDEST SINGLE TREE IN THE WORLD IS A BRISTLECONE PINE IN CALIFORNIA, CALLED METHUSELAH. IT'S MORE THAN 4,850 YEARS OLD. MAKE UP A STORY ABOUT SOMETHING THE TREE HAS SEEN IN ITS LONG LIFE.

51. IN THE PALUXY RIVER IN TEXAS, YOU CAN WALK WHERE DINOSAURS WALKED, PUTTING YOUR FEET INTO THEIR FOSSILIZED FOOTSTEPS. DRAW YOUR FOOTPRINTS INSIDE THIS DINO PRINT.

152. MANY CITIES AND TOWNS HAVE FOUNTAINS. SOME ARE TALL, SPURTING COLUMNS OF WATER. OTHERS INVOLVE FANCY SCULPTURES. DESIGN YOUR OWN FOUNTAIN HERE.

153.

IMAGINE THAT ALIENS CAME TO YOUR COUNTRY FOR A VACATION. WHAT ARE THEY MOST EXCITED TO SEE OR DO?

154.

LONDON BRIDGE ONCE SPANNED THE RIVER THAMES IN LONDON, ENGLAND. IN 1968, IT WAS BOUGHT BY LAKE HAVASU CITY, ARIZONA, AND MOVED THERE STONE BY STONE. WHICH MONUMENT WOULD YOU MOVE AND WHERE WOULD YOU PUT IT?

155.

THE SKELETON COAST IN NAMIBIA IS LITTERED WITH SHIPWRECKS. YOU CAN EVEN STAY IN SOME AS HOTELS. WHAT WOULD YOU LIKE TO DO AMONG THE SHIPWRECKS?

156.

CHRISTMAS ISLAND, AUSTRALIA, IS HOME TO A BRIDGE BUILT TO HELP THE ISLAND'S RED CRABS CROSS THE ROAD SAFELY. WHAT ANIMAL WOULD YOU BUILD A BRIDGE FOR NEAR YOU?

157.

LAKE MARACAIBO, VENEZUELA, IS STRUCK BY LIGHTNING MORE THAN
ANY OTHER REGION IN THE WORLD—SOMETIMES 40,000 TIMES A NIGHT!
FILL THIS SKY WITH A DRAMATIC LIGHTNING STORM.

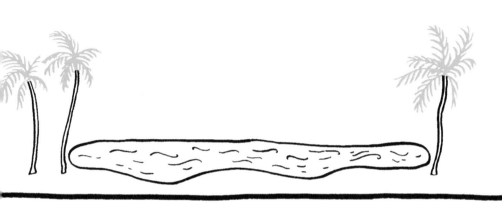

158.

ZEDIS ARE SACRED BUILDINGS IN BUDDHISM, SHAPED LIKE MOUNDS
WITH TALL TOWERS ON TOP. AT A LAKE NEAR SHWE INDEIN,
MYANMAR, THERE ARE OVER 1,000 ZEDIS, SOME OF WHICH ARE
AROUND 400 YEARS OLD. ADD SOME MORE ZEDIS TO THIS SCENE.

159.

A HOUSE IN DRESDEN, GERMANY, HAS A MAZE OF FUNNELS AND PIPES ALL OVER THE OUTSIDE. WHEN RAIN FALLS, IT MAKES MUSIC AS IT RUSHES THROUGH THE "FUNNEL WALL." DESIGN YOUR OWN FUNNEL WALL FOR THE HOUSE NEXT DOOR.

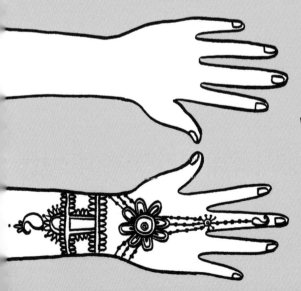

160.

BRIDES AT TRADITIONAL HINDU WEDDINGS WEAR MEHNDI, DECORATIVE PATTERNS DRAWN ON THE HANDS AND ARMS WITH A DYE CALLED HENNA. DECORATE THIS BRIDE'S OTHER HAND.

161.

AT 2,150 MILES, THE GREAT WALL OF CHINA IS THE WORLD'S LONGEST WALL.
IT WAS STARTED 2,200 YEARS AGO AND ADDED TO OVER CENTURIES.
ADD YOUR OWN SECTION TO THE WALL HERE.

162.

THE LARGEST SECONDHAND BOOK MARKET IN THE WORLD IS ON COLLEGE
STREET IN KOLKATA, INDIA. IT'S OVER 1 MILE LONG. WRITE A SHORT STORY
ABOUT FINDING A SPECIAL BOOK THERE. WHAT IS IT CALLED?
WHAT IS IT ABOUT? WHO DID IT BELONG TO?

163.

THE MORAKI BOULDERS ARE GIANT, NATURALLY EGG-SHAPED STONES ON KOEKOHE BEACH, IN NEW ZEALAND. DRAW WHAT WOULD HATCH FROM THEM IF THEY ACTUALLY WERE EGGS.

164.

CAÑO CRISTALES IN COLOMBIA IS ALSO CALLED THE "LIQUID RAINBOW." THE RIVER CHANGES COLOR WHEN CERTAIN PLANTS GROW IN IT. COLOR IT IN.

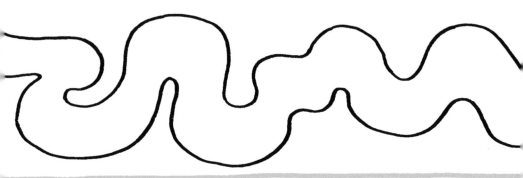

165.

DURING THE SUMMER, VISITORS FLOCK TO THE VALLEY OF FLOWERS IN UTTARAKHAND, INDIA, WHERE 600 DIFFERENT TYPES OF FLOWERS GROW. DRAW COLORFUL FLOWERS ALL OVER THE GRASS IN THE VALLEY.

166.

THE GOLDEN BRIDGE IN HÒA VANG, VIETNAM, IS SUPPORTED BY TWO GIANT HANDS CARVED OUT OF STONE. DRAW WHO THEY BELONG TO.

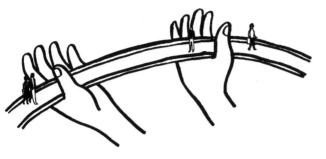

167.

IN SOUTH KOREA, THERE'S A THEME PARK DEDICATED TO CHEESE! IF YOU COULD BUILD A THEME PARK ALL ABOUT ONE FOOD, WHAT FOOD WOULD IT BE AND WHAT WOULD YOU CALL YOUR PARK?

168.

IF YOU COULD TRAVEL BY ANY MEANS TO GO ON AN AMAZING VACATION, WHAT WOULD YOU CHOOSE?

169.

MANY CITIES AROUND THE WORLD HAVE SUBWAY SYSTEMS FOR
PEOPLE TO TRAVEL UNDERGROUND. FILL THIS UNDERGROUND
AREA WITH TUNNELS, TRAINS, AND PEOPLE.

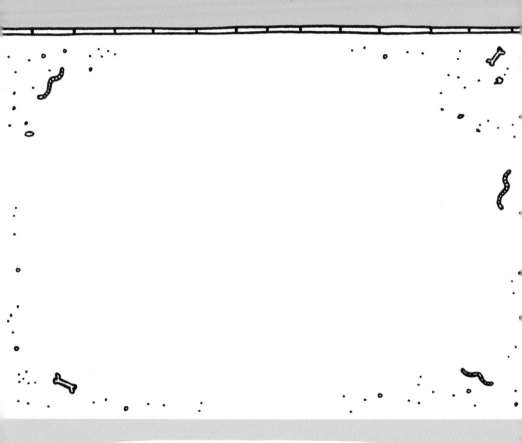

170.

DO YOU SPEAK MORE THAN ONE LANGUAGE? IF YOU COULD
LEARN A NEW ONE, WHAT WOULD IT BE, AND WHY?

171.

THE SUMMER OLYMPIC GAMES HAPPEN EVERY FOUR YEARS IN A DIFFERENT CITY. A FLAMING TORCH IS LIT IN OLYMPIA, GREECE, THEN CARRIED TO THE HOST CITY OF THE NEXT GAMES. DRAW YOURSELF RUNNING WITH THE OLYMPIC FLAME THROUGH YOUR HOMETOWN.

172.

CAMPING VACATIONS COME IN ALL SHAPES AND SIZES. IN KENYA, YOU CAN SLEEP IN A LUXURY TREEHOUSE, WHILE IN THE NETHERLANDS, YOU CAN CAMP ON A FLOATING RAFT! DESIGN AN AMAZING TENT YOU'D LIKE TO STAY IN.

173.

SOME COUNTRIES HAVE FOLK COSTUMES OR CEREMONIAL DRESS, WHICH PEOPLE WEAR FOR SPECIAL OCCASIONS. DESIGN AN OUTFIT FOR YOU TO WEAR ON YOUR BIRTHDAY EVERY YEAR.

174.

DURING THE SUMMER, IN PARTS OF THE WORLD IN THE ARCTIC CIRCLE, SUCH AS CANADA, ICELAND, AND GREENLAND, THE SUN DOESN'T SET FOR ABOUT THREE MONTHS. WHAT WOULD YOU DO WITH 24 HOURS OF SUNLIGHT EVERY DAY?

175.

VISITORS TO LAS VEGAS, NEVADA, ARE WELCOMED BY A FAMOUS NEON SIGN. REWRITE THE SIGN SO IT WELCOMES VISITORS TO YOUR HOMETOWN.

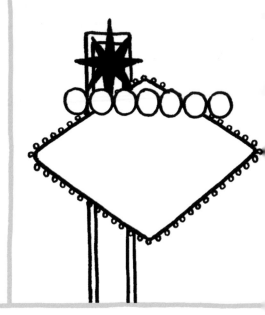

176.

THE GREAT SPHINX OF GIZA IS A 4,500-YEAR-OLD MONUMENT IN EGYPT, WITH THE FACE OF A HUMAN AND THE BODY OF A LION. BUT IT'S MISSING ITS NOSE! MAKE UP A STORY ABOUT WHAT HAPPENED TO IT.

177.

THE ARMADILLO IN GLASGOW, SCOTLAND, IS A BUILDING THAT RESEMBLES THE ARMOR OF AN ARMADILLO. DESIGN A BUILDING THAT LOOKS LIKE YOUR FAVORITE ANIMAL.

178.

THE AQUARELLE TRAIN IS PART OF THE METRO SYSTEM OF MOSCOW, RUSSIA. IT'S A MOVING ART GALLERY, FILLED WITH WATERCOLOR PAINTINGS IN DECORATIVE FRAMES. WHAT UNEXPECTED PLACE WOULD YOU PUT AN ART GALLERY IN?

179.

A GROUP OF STRANGELY TWISTED PINE TREES GROWS IN A FOREST NEAR GRYFINO, POLAND. THE OTHER TREES NEARBY ARE STRAIGHT. MAKE UP A REASON TO EXPLAIN WHY THEY ARE LIKE THIS.

180.

BOTANICAL GARDENS ARE PLACES WHERE UNUSUAL AND INTERESTING PLANTS ARE GROWN FOR THE PUBLIC TO VISIT, SUCH AS KEW GARDENS IN ENGLAND. FILL THIS GREENHOUSE WITH AMAZING PLANTS.

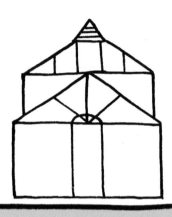

181.

THE CITY OF SÃO PAULO, BRAZIL, ONCE ELECTED A RHINOCEROS CALLED CACARECO AS THEIR COUNCILOR. WHAT ANIMAL POLITICIAN WOULD GET YOUR VOTE?

182.

NOVEMBER 23RD IS LABOR THANKSGIVING DAY IN JAPAN. CHILDREN GIVE CARDS AND GIFTS TO PEOPLE WHOSE HARD WORK HELPS THEM, SUCH AS POLICE OFFICERS, FIREFIGHTERS, AND NURSES. WHO WOULD YOU THANK?

183.

IN THE CARIBBEAN, PEOPLE GO TO BEACHES TO WATCH SEA TURTLES HATCH. ADD SOME BABY SEA TURTLES MAKING THEIR WAY TO THE OCEAN FROM THE BEACH.

184.

IN IRAN, ICE CREAM IS SOMETIMES SERVED WITH NOODLES. IN CHINA, ICED TEA ICE CREAM CAN BE FRIED IN BATTER. INVENT A NEW WAY TO SERVE ICE CREAM.

185.

WHEN SOME PEOPLE IN THE PHILIPPINES MOVE, THEY ACTUALLY MOVE THEIR HOUSE! THEY TIE BAMBOO POLES BENEATH IT AND CARRY THE HOUSE TO A NEW PLACE. WHERE WOULD YOU LIKE TO MOVE YOUR HOME TO?

186.

MAGNETIC HILL IN LADAKH, INDIA, ATTRACTS METAL OBJECTS—IT'S A GIANT MAGNET! IMAGINE YOU DROVE THERE AND GOT OUT FOR A WALK. THEN, YOUR CAR IS SLOWLY DRAWN TO THE HILL. WHAT HAPPENS NEXT?

187.

EVERY FEW YEARS, A NEW, TEMPORARY ARTWORK IS PLACED ON THE FOURTH PLINTH IN TRAFALGAR SQUARE, IN LONDON, ENGLAND. PREVIOUS WORKS HAVE INCLUDED A GIANT THUMBS-UP AND A SCOOP OF ICE CREAM. PUT YOUR OWN ARTWORK ON THE PLINTH BELOW.

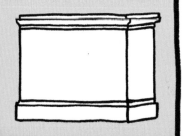

188.

IN LAPLAND, FINLAND, YOU CAN SPEND THE NIGHT IN A DOME MADE ENTIRELY OF GLASS. WHAT WOULD BE GOOD AND BAD ABOUT STAYING IN A SEE-THROUGH BUILDING?

189.

THE HOLLYWOOD WALK OF FAME IN LOS ANGELES, CALIFORNIA, HAS STARS SET INTO THE SIDEWALK, MANY WITH THE NAMES OF FAMOUS MOVIE OR MUSIC STARS. FILL IN STARS FOR THREE PERFORMERS YOU ADMIRE.

190.

THE RAKOTZBRÜCKE BRIDGE IN GABLENZ, GERMANY, FORMS A PERFECT CIRCLE WITH ITS REFLECTION IN THE WATER. DRAW THE BRIDGE'S REFLECTION.

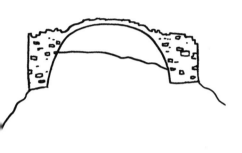

191.

ELVES ARE AN IMPORTANT PART OF ICELANDIC FOLKLORE—SO MUCH SO THAT SOME PEOPLE BUILD MINIATURE HOUSES FOR THEM TO LIVE IN. DESIGN AN ELF HOUSE HERE.

192.

POINT NEMO IS A SPOT IN THE MIDDLE OF THE PACIFIC OCEAN THAT IS FARTHER FROM LAND THAN ANY OTHER POINT ON EARTH. DESIGN AN AD FOR A CRUISE TO POINT NEMO.

193.

THE HOUSES OF TIÉBÉLÉ IN BURKINA FASO ARE MADE OF NATURAL MATERIALS AND HAND DECORATED WITH BEAUTIFUL GEOMETRIC PATTERNS. FINISH DECORATING THIS HOUSE.

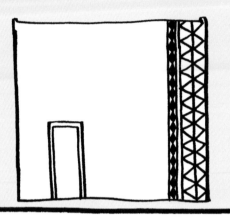

194.

AN ARCHIPELAGO IS A CLUSTER OF ISLANDS. DRAW A LOT OF SMALL ISLANDS HERE AND GIVE THEM ALL NAMES.

195.

ONE WAY TO GET A TASTE OF A NEW PLACE IS TO EAT THE STREET FOOD SOLD THERE, FROM FILLED PASTRIES CALLED EMPANADAS IN ARGENTINA, TO BÁNH MÌ BAGUETTES IN VIETNAM. DECORATE THIS STREET-FOOD STAND SELLING YOUR FAVORITE SNACKS.

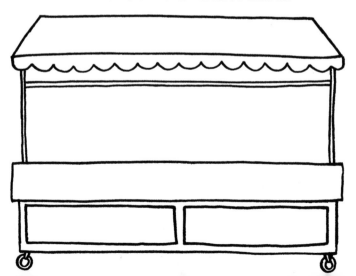

196.

AT 420 MILES, MAMMOTH CAVE NATIONAL PARK IN KENTUCKY IS THE LONGEST CAVE SYSTEM IN THE WORLD. DRAW SOME UNDERGROUND CAVES HERE, SHOWING WHAT'S INSIDE AND HOW THEY'RE CONNECTED.

197.

THE HINDU SRI RANGANATHASWAMY TEMPLE IN INDIA IS PAINTED IN ALL THE COLORS OF THE RAINBOW. COLOR IT IN AS BRIGHTLY AS YOU CAN.

198.

KAYASHIMA RAILWAY STATION IN JAPAN IS BUILT AROUND A 700-YEAR-OLD TREE. THE TREE WAS IN THE WAY—BUT LOCAL PEOPLE SAID CUTTING IT DOWN WOULD BRING BAD LUCK. DRAW A BUILDING AROUND THIS TREE.

199. THE CHOCOLATE HILLS IN THE PHILIPPINES GET THEIR NAME FROM THE BROWN COLOR THEY BECOME IN THE DRY SEASON. MAKE UP A SILLIER REASON FOR THE NAME.

200. WILLASTON IN ENGLAND IS HOST TO AN ANNUAL WORM-CHARMING COMPETITION. PEOPLE PLAY MUSIC, SING, AND JUMP UP AND DOWN ON THE GROUND TO MAKE EARTHWORMS COME TO THE SURFACE. HOW WOULD YOU COAX SOME WORMS UP FROM UNDERGROUND?

201. IN BERMUDA, A COUPLE GETTING MARRIED WALKS THROUGH A CIRCULAR "MOON GATE," WHICH THEY BELIEVE BRINGS GOOD LUCK. INVENT A TRADITION TO BRING GOOD LUCK.

202. IN THE KARAKUM DESERT, IN TURKMENISTAN, THERE'S A HOLE FILLED WITH GAS THAT IS PERMANENTLY ON FIRE. FILL THIS ONE WITH SOMETHING UNEXPECTED.

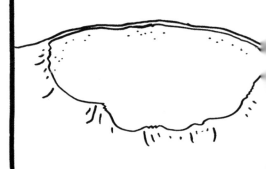

203. BARCELONA, SPAIN, WAS HOME TO THE ARCHITECT GAUDI, WHO MADE BUILDINGS IN BRIGHT COLORS AND WITH CURVED, WOBBLY LINES WHERE THERE ARE USUALLY STRAIGHT LINES. DRAW A WIBBLY-WOBBLY VERSION OF YOUR OWN HOME.

204. SOCOTRA, OFF THE COAST OF YEMEN, IS KNOWN FOR ITS MANY UNIQUE TREE SPECIES THAT DON'T GROW ANYWHERE ELSE ON EARTH. MAKE UP A NEW UNUSUAL TREE TO GO WITH THE ONES BELOW.

CUCUMBER TREE

DRAGON'S BLOOD TREE

205.

THE PARTHENON IS AN ANCIENT, RUINED TEMPLE IN ATHENS, GREECE. PARTS OF IT HAVE BEEN REBUILT TO KEEP IT STANDING. MAKE THE PARTHENON WHOLE AGAIN BY DRAWING THE REST HOWEVER YOU LIKE.

206.

KING LUDWIG OF BAVARIA (SOUTH GERMANY) BUILT SEVERAL CASTLES, MAKING THEM AS FANCY AS POSSIBLE. THE CASTLE AT DISNEYLAND IS BASED ON HIS NEUSCHWANSTEIN CASTLE. DESIGN YOUR OWN FANCY CASTLE HERE.

207.

LAKE NATRON IN TANZANIA IS TOXIC TO HUMANS, BUT FLAMINGOS LOVE IT! MOST OF THE WORLD'S LESSER FLAMINGOS FLY THERE EVERY YEAR TO BREED. FILL THIS LAKE WITH PINK FLAMINGOS.

208.

GRUB'S UP! PEOPLE EAT INSECTS ALL OVER THE WORLD, FROM CRUNCHY CHAPULINES (FRIED GRASSHOPPERS) IN MEXICO TO SPICY BOTOK TAWON (STEAMED BEE LARVAE) IN INDONESIA. INVENT A CREEPY-CRAWLY DISH OF YOUR OWN.

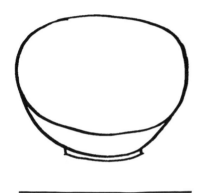

209.

IN PARTS OF ASIA, PEOPLE TRADITIONALLY BURN INCENSE TO RELEASE PLEASANT SMELLS. WHICH SMELLS WOULD YOU CHOOSE TO MAKE YOU CALM AND HAPPY?

210.

THREE COUNTRIES IN THE WORLD HAVE A DRAGON ON THEIR NATIONAL FLAG: WALES, MALTA, AND BHUTAN. DRAW A NEW DRAGON TO GO ON YOUR COUNTRY'S FLAG.

211.

THE WORLD'S SMALLEST COUNTRY IS VATICAN CITY, WITH FEWER THAN 1,000 INHABITANTS. INVENT AN EVEN SMALLER COUNTRY. WHAT'S IT CALLED AND HOW MANY PEOPLE LIVE THERE?

212.

JELLYFISH LAKE ON THE PACIFIC ISLAND OF PALAU IS HOME
TO MILLIONS OF JELLYFISH, AND TOURISTS VISIT TO SWIM
AMONG THEM. WHAT DO YOU THINK IT WOULD BE
LIKE TO SWIM IN A LAKE OF JELLYFISH?

213.

IN COYOACÁN, MEXICO, YOU CAN VISIT THE HOUSE OF ARTIST FRIDA KAHLO,
AND IN BERN, SWITZERLAND, THE APARTMENT WHERE SCIENTIST ALBERT
EINSTEIN ONCE LIVED IS OPEN TO THE PUBLIC. WHICH HISTORICAL FIGURE'S
HOME WOULD YOU LIKE TO VISIT IF YOU COULD?

214.

SHARM EL-SHEIKH, IN EGYPT, IS HOME TO ONE OF THE WORLD'S LARGEST
SWIMMING POOLS. THE 24-ACRE LAGOON IS AT A RESORT THREE MILES INLAND,
IN THE MIDDLE OF THE SINAI DESERT. WHAT WOULD YOU LIKE TO DO THERE?

215.

THE ATACAMA DESERT, IN SOUTH AMERICA, HAS BEEN USED IN NASA EXPERIMENTS DUE TO ITS SIMILARITY TO THE PLANET MARS. IT'S CERTAINLY HOME TO SOME OTHERWORLDLY SIGHTS, LIKE A ROCK THAT RESEMBLES A TREE. FILL THE DESERT WITH MORE STONE TREES.

216.

TINTAGEL CASTLE IS A RUIN IN CORNWALL, ENGLAND. BUILD A CASTLE OF YOUR OWN ON THE RUINS OF TINTAGEL.

217.

MANY COUNTRIES HAVE A NATIONAL ANTHEM: A SONG THAT'S SUNG AT OFFICIAL EVENTS AND CEREMONIES. SOME ARE HUNDREDS OF YEARS OLD, WHILE OTHERS ARE MORE RECENT. WHAT SONG WOULD YOU PICK AS YOUR COUNTRY'S NEW NATIONAL ANTHEM?

_____

_____

_____

_____

_____

218.

PEOPLE TRAVEL TO THE COAST OF NORTHUMBERLAND, IN ENGLAND, TO SEE THE MANY PUFFINS THAT NEST ON THE CLIFFS. WHICH TYPE OF BIRD WOULD YOU LIKE TO SEE IN THE WILD?

219.

SIGHTSEERS GATHER AT THE SOUTHERN EDGE OF THE PERITO MORENO GLACIER, IN ARGENTINA, TO WATCH ENORMOUS CHUNKS OF ICE DETACH AND FALL AROUND 240 FEET INTO THE WATER. IMAGINE THAT YOU SEE THIS HAPPEN— DESCRIBE IT IN ONE SENTENCE.

220.

PEOPLE VISITING SANDY BEACHES OFTEN MAKE SANDCASTLES OR SAND SCULPTURES. DESIGN YOUR OWN SANDCASTLE HERE.

221.

BHUTAN'S BLACK-NECKED CRANE FESTIVAL CELEBRATES THE ELEGANT BIRDS THAT MIGRATE TO BHUTAN JUST AS THE HARVEST SEASON ENDS. WHAT ANIMAL WOULD YOU DEDICATE A FESTIVAL TO?

222.

PETRA IS AN ANCIENT CITY IN JORDAN, CARVED OUT OF THE
ROSE-COLORED ROCK. DRAW SOME CLIFFS HERE, THEN TURN THEM INTO A CITY.

223.

THE LIBERTY BELL IS AN ICONIC US SYMBOL IN PHILADELPHIA,
PENNSYLVANIA. IT'S FAMOUS FOR A LARGE CRACK THAT FORMED IN THE
19TH CENTURY. MAKE UP A STORY ABOUT HOW THE BELL BECAME CRACKED.

224.

THE SS *AYRFIELD* IS A RUSTED, ABANDONED SHIP FLOATING IN HOMEBUSH BAY, AUSTRALIA. IT'S COMPLETELY OVERGROWN WITH TREES AND PLANT LIFE. WRITE A STORY ABOUT EXPLORING THIS MYSTERIOUS FLOATING FOREST.

225.

THERE'S A "UFO WELCOME CENTER" IN BOWMAN, SOUTH CAROLINA, BUILT BY A SPACE ENTHUSIAST. WHAT WOULD YOU SAY TO WELCOME AN ALIEN VISITOR?

226.

THE CITY OF COPENHAGEN, IN DENMARK, HAS A ROAD CALLED POTATO ROW, WHICH USED TO BE A POTATO FIELD. MAKE UP FIVE FUNNY ROAD NAMES.

1. _ _ _ _ _ _ _ _ _ _ _

2. _ _ _ _ _ _ _ _ _ _ _

3. _ _ _ _ _ _ _ _ _ _ _

4. _ _ _ _ _ _ _ _ _ _ _

5. _ _ _ _ _ _ _ _ _ _ _

227.

ANGEL FALLS, IN VENEZUELA, IS THE WORLD'S HIGHEST WATERFALL—IT'S SO TALL THAT, DURING THE WARM MONTHS, MOST OF ITS WATER EVAPORATES BEFORE IT HITS THE GROUND! DRAW A PLUNGING WATERFALL DOWN THE SIDE OF THIS CLIFF.

228.

AMONG OTHER THINGS, THE NETHERLANDS IS FAMOUS FOR ITS MANY OLD WOODEN WINDMILLS. DRAW A WINDMILL BELOW.

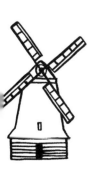

229.

IN YANCHENG, CHINA, THERE'S A HEDGE MAZE WITH OVER FIVE MILES OF WINDING PATHS. DESIGN YOUR OWN MAZE HERE—DON'T GET LOST!

230.

AT SALAR DE UYUNI, A VAST EXPANSE OF FLAT, SALT-COVERED GROUND IN BOLIVIA, A SHALLOW LAYER OF WATER FORMS WHEN IT RAINS, TURNING IT INTO A GIANT MIRROR. TOURISTS TAKE PHOTOS POSING WITH THEIR REFLECTIONS. DRAW YOURSELF STANDING IN THE WATER, AND YOUR REFLECTION BELOW.

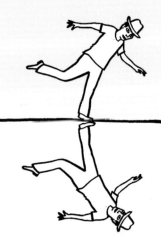

231.

HARBIN ICE FESTIVAL TAKES PLACE IN CHINA IN JANUARY AND FEBRUARY EACH YEAR. VISITORS CAN EXPLORE ENTIRE BUILDINGS, SCULPTURES, AND EVEN RESTAURANTS BUILT FROM ICE. DESIGN AN ICE SCULPTURE FOR THE FESTIVAL.

232.

A TAJINE IS A CLAY POT USED IN MOROCCO TO COOK A DISH OF THE SAME NAME. THEY ARE OFTEN DECORATED WITH INTRICATE AND COLORFUL PATTERNS. DECORATE THIS TAJINE.

233.

TEX-MEX IS A TYPE OF FOOD THAT COMBINES TEXAN AND MEXICAN STYLES OF COOKING. DESCRIBE OR DRAW YOUR OWN CUISINE COMBINING THE STYLES OF TWO PLACES. WHAT IS YOUR FAVORITE DISH?

234.

TSINGY DE BEMARAHA IS A NATIONAL PARK IN MADAGASCAR, FILLED WITH LARGE, NEEDLE-SHARP LIMESTONE BOULDERS. MAKE UP FOUR RULES TO HELP PEOPLE STAY SAFE NEAR THE POINTY ROCKS.

1. _____

_____

_____

_____

2. _____

_____

_____

_____

3. _____

_____

_____

_____

4. _____

_____

_____

_____

235.

BENEATH THE STREETS OF PARIS, FRANCE, IS A NETWORK OF STORAGE CHAMBERS FOR HUMAN SKELETONS. THEY WERE BUILT IN THE 1700S WHEN THE CITY'S CEMETERIES WERE FULL. WRITE A FRIGHTENING STORY ABOUT SPENDING THE NIGHT THERE.

236.

CRUISE SHIPS ARE FLOATING HOTELS AND RESORTS, TAKING PASSENGERS ON VACATIONS AROUND THE WORLD. DECORATE THIS CRUISE SHIP AND WRITE ITS NAME ON THE SIDE.

237.

IN ROMANIA, FARMERS GATHER THEIR HAY INTO UNUSUALLY SHAPED STACKS. TURN THESE ROMANIAN HAYSTACKS INTO MADE-UP CREATURES.

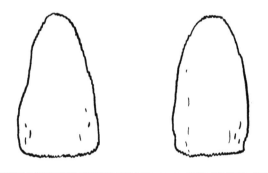

238.

YOU CAN GO WHITEWATER RAFTING ON THE ZAMBEZI RIVER IN SOUTHERN AFRICA. CREWS OF SIX NAVIGATE A SMALL RAFT THROUGH THUNDERING RIVER RAPIDS, PASSING BEAUTIFUL SCENERY AS THEY GO. WOULD YOU WANT TO TRY? WHY OR WHY NOT?

_____

_____

_____

_____

239.

DURING VERY COLD WINTERS, THE CANALS OF AMSTERDAM, IN THE NETHERLANDS, FREEZE OVER, AND PEOPLE SKATE ON THE ICE. ADD PEOPLE TO THIS ICY CANAL TO TURN IT INTO A FROZEN WONDERLAND.

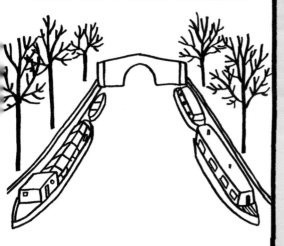

240.

IN PAPUA NEW GUINEA, THERE ARE AROUND 840 DIFFERENT LANGUAGES— THE MOST OF ANY COUNTRY IN THE WORLD. DO YOU KNOW HOW TO SAY "HELLO" IN MORE THAN ONE LANGUAGE? WRITE "HELLO" IN AS MANY LANGUAGES AS YOU CAN THINK OF.

241.

AT THE SUMMIT OF MOUNT KILIMANJARO, IN TANZANIA, THERE'S A SIGN CONGRATULATING CLIMBERS WHO MAKE IT TO THE TOP. WRITE A MESSAGE OF CONGRATULATIONS ON THIS SIGN.

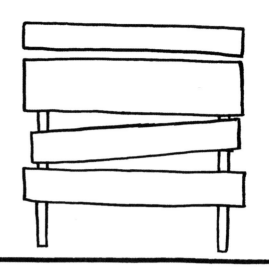

242.

SOME COUNTRIES USE MUSICAL INSTRUMENTS AS NATIONAL SYMBOLS, SUCH AS THE STEELPAN DRUM OF TRINIDAD AND TOBAGO OR THE KOTO, A LARGE STRINGED INSTRUMENT FROM JAPAN. WHAT INSTRUMENT WOULD YOU PICK TO REPRESENT YOUR COUNTRY?

243.

AT COLOMBIA'S SAN AGUSTÍN ARCHAEOLOGICAL PARK, THERE ARE LARGE STATUES OF HUMANS, MONSTERS, AND ANIMALS. LITTLE IS KNOWN ABOUT THE PEOPLE WHO MADE THEM 1,500 YEARS AGO. ADD YOUR OWN STATUE IN A SIMILAR STYLE.

244. PEOPLE TRAVEL TO THE FAR NORTH TO SEE THE AURORA BOREALIS: NATURAL SWIRLS OF COLORFUL LIGHT THAT OCCUR IN THE NIGHT SKY, CLOSE TO EARTH'S POLES. THEY'RE CAUSED BY CHARGED PARTICLES IN EARTH'S ATMOSPHERE. FILL THIS SKY WITH A BRILLIANT LIGHT DISPLAY.

245. TRUFFLES ARE FUNGI THAT GROW UNDERGROUND, AT THE BASE OF TREES. A PRIZED INGREDIENT IN FANCY RESTAURANTS, THEY ARE FOUND IN EUROPE, NORTH AMERICA, AND AUSTRALIA, WHERE TRAINED DOGS SNIFF THEM OUT. DRAW SOME DOGS SNIFFING FOR TRUFFLES IN THIS FOREST.

246. IN BAKAU, GAMBIA, THERE IS A SACRED POOL OPEN TO VISITORS ... AND FILLED WITH CROCODILES! THESE PAMPERED CROCS ARE SO TAME, YOU CAN WALK RIGHT UP AND PET THEM. DRAW YOURSELF VISITING SOME CROCODILES.

247. IN 1883, THE VOLCANO KRAKATAU, IN INDONESIA, ERUPTED SO POWERFULLY THAT IT WAS HEARD 3,000 MILES AWAY, AND TURNED THE SKY RED FOR MONTHS. WRITE A NEWSPAPER HEADLINE ANNOUNCING THE DRAMATIC ERUPTION.

248. THE WAITOMO CAVES IN NEW ZEALAND ARE AN UNDERGROUND NETWORK OF TUNNELS, CAVES, LAKES, AND HOLES—ALL LIT UP BY SHINY BLUE-GREEN GLOWWORMS. ADD GLOWWORMS TO THIS ROCKY SCENE.

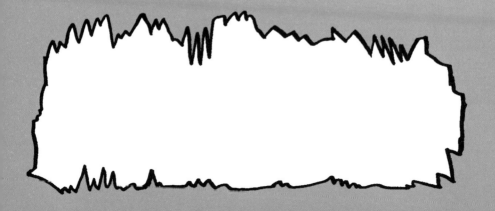

249.

YOU'RE SCUBA DIVING IN AUSTRALIA, OVER THE GREAT BARRIER REEF—
THE LARGEST CORAL REEF IN THE WORLD! DRAW THE SIGHTS YOU SEE.

250.

IN LUCERNE, SWITZERLAND, YOU CAN VISIT A GLACIER GARDEN AND SEE
STRANGE ROCK FORMATIONS CREATED BY ICE MOVING AND MELTING 20,000
YEARS AGO. WRITE A DIARY ENTRY DESCRIBING LIFE IN THE ICE AGE.

251.

NAADAM IS A MONGOLIAN SPORTS FESTIVAL DURING WHICH PEOPLE COMPETE AT THREE TRADITIONAL ACTIVITIES: WRESTLING, ARCHERY, AND HORSE RACING. WHAT THREE SPORTS WOULD YOU INCLUDE AT A NATIONAL FESTIVAL?

_____

_____

_____

252.

THE GNOME RESERVE IN DEVON, ENGLAND, IS HOME TO 2,000 GARDEN GNOMES. DESIGN YOUR OWN GARDEN GNOME TO ADD TO THE COLLECTION.

253.

IN MEXICO, IT'S TRADITIONAL TO PUSH SOMEONE'S FACE INTO THEIR BIRTHDAY CAKE. DRAW A NICE BIRTHDAY CAKE, READY FOR THIS TO HAPPEN.

254.

COWS ARE SUCH AN IMPORTANT PART OF LIFE IN RWANDA THAT PEOPLE GO TO BARS THAT ONLY SERVE MILK. IF YOU OWNED A RESTAURANT THAT COULD ONLY SERVE ONE THING, WHAT WOULD IT BE?

255.

SLOPE POINT IN NEW ZEALAND IS ONE OF THE WINDIEST PLACES IN THE WORLD. THE TREES LEAN OVER, CONSTANTLY BLASTED BY WINDS FROM ANTARCTICA. DRAW SOME WINDBLOWN TREES ON THIS HILLTOP.

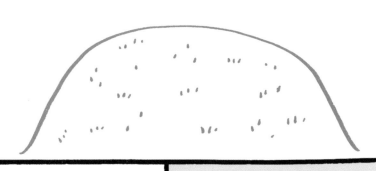

256.

WHEN THEIR BABY TEETH FALL OUT, CHILDREN IN GREECE MAKE A WISH AND THROW THEM ONTO THE ROOF! INVENT A FUNNY THING TO DO WITH YOUR BABY TEETH.

257.

THE DOORWAY RAILWAY IN HANOI, VIETNAM, GOES ALONG A NARROW STREET, FORCING PEOPLE TO SQUEEZE AGAINST THE WALLS WHEN IT PASSES. IF A TRAIN CAME TO YOUR DOOR, WHERE WOULD YOU LIKE IT TO TAKE YOU?

258.

AT PUNTA DEL ESTE, URUGUAY, A SCULPTURE OF A GIANT HAND APPEARS
TO BE BURIED IN THE SAND. TRACE AROUND YOUR HAND IN THIS SPACE,
THEN DRAW A SCENE AROUND IT TO MAKE IT LOOK LIKE A SCULPTURE.

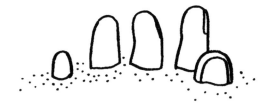

259.

THE NAZCA LINES IN PERU ARE HUGE PICTURES OF ANIMALS, BUGS, AND SYMBOLS SCRATCHED INTO THE DESERT. THEY ARE 1,500–2,500 YEARS OLD. NO ONE KNOWS EXACTLY WHY THEY WERE MADE. WHAT'S YOUR THEORY?

260.

JAPAN'S MEIJI CHOCOLATE FACTORY IS DESIGNED TO LOOK LIKE—WHAT ELSE?— A GIANT BAR OF CHOCOLATE! DESIGN A FACTORY SHAPED LIKE WHAT IT MAKES.

261.

HUNDREDS OF GIANT, MAN-MADE STONE JARS ARE SCATTERED ACROSS XIENG KHOUANG IN LAOS. ONE LEGEND SAYS THEY WERE USED TO BREW DRINKS FOR GIANTS. MAKE UP A RECIPE FOR A GIANT'S BREW.

262.

LEGEND TELLS OF PIRATE TREASURE BURIED IN A "MONEY PIT" ON OAK ISLAND, IN CANADA. TURN THIS DRAWING OF THE ISLAND INTO A TREASURE MAP— REMEMBER, X MARKS THE SPOT!

263.

THERE IS A STEEL BRIDGE IN AMSTERDAM THAT WASN'T BUILT LIKE MOST BRIDGES—IT WAS 3D PRINTED! IF YOU COULD 3D PRINT ANY TYPE OF STRUCTURE OR BUILDING FOR WHERE YOU LIVE, WHAT WOULD IT BE?

264.

IN SPAIN, CHILDREN LEAVE OUT SHOES ON THE NIGHT BEFORE THE EPIPHANY. IN THE MORNING, THEY FIND THE SHOES FILLED WITH GIFTS! DRAW GIFTS IN THESE SHOES.

265. DALLOL, ETHIOPIA, IS THE HOTTEST PLACE WHERE PEOPLE LIVE ON EARTH, WITH AN AVERAGE TEMPERATURE OF 94.3°F. WRITE DOWN FIVE THINGS YOU WOULD USE OR DO TO KEEP COOL IF YOU LIVED THERE.

1. _ _ _ _ _ _ _   2. _ _ _ _ _ _

3. _ _ _ _ _ _ _ _   4. _ _ _ _ _ _

5. _ _ _ _ _ _ _

266. SOME PEOPLE BELIEVE A DINOSAUR-LIKE MONSTER CALLED MOKELE-MBEMBE LIVES IN A LAKE IN THE REPUBLIC OF CONGO. WHAT DO YOU THINK IT LOOKS LIKE? DRAW IT HERE.

267. IN DEATH VALLEY, CALIFORNIA, "SAILING STONES" MOVE ACROSS THE DESERT, LEAVING LONG TRAILS BEHIND THEM. THEY'RE DRIVEN BY MELTING SHEETS OF ICE BEING BLOWN BY THE WIND. MAKE UP A DIFFERENT REASON WHY THE ROCKS MOVE.

268. AT THE FLOATING MARKETS OF BANGKOK, THAILAND, ALL THE STALLS ARE BOATS. THEY SELL FRUIT, VEGETABLES, FLOWERS, AND TASTY HOT FOOD. DRAW SOME THINGS FOR SALE ON THIS BOAT.

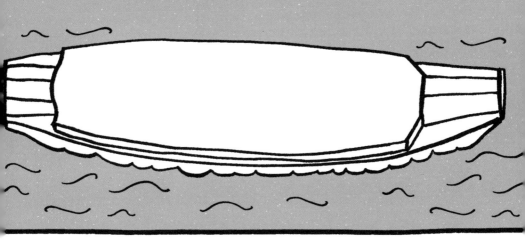

269. A GROUP OF TALL BLACK ROCKS IN THE SEA NEAR ICELAND ARE SAID TO BE TROLLS TURNED TO STONE AS THEY TRIED TO DRAG A SHIP TO SHORE. WRITE A LEGEND TO EXPLAIN A LANDMARK YOU KNOW.

270.

THE NATURALLY WARM, MINERAL-RICH WATERS OF THE BLUE LAGOON IN ICELAND ARE SUPPOSED TO BE GOOD FOR YOUR SKIN. COLOR THE LAGOON SO IT LIVES UP TO ITS NAME.

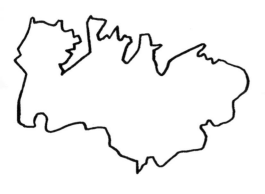

271.

BAIGALMAA NORJMAA SET OUT TO TRAVEL 7,500 MILES FROM MONGOLIA TO ENGLAND BY CAMEL. PLAN YOUR OWN AMBITIOUS JOURNEY.

272.

ARGENTINA IS HOME TO THE WORLD'S LARGEST SAND DUNE, AT OVER 4,000 FEET TALL. WHAT WOULD YOU LIKE TO DO ON A HILL OF SAND?

273.

LAS POZAS IS AN OUTDOOR MUSEUM IN MEXICO, DEEP IN THE RAIN FOREST. IT'S FILLED WITH SCULPTURES OF CRUMBLING BUILDINGS AND GIANT HANDS, BUILT IN THE 20TH CENTURY. ADD SOME SCULPTURES TO THIS JUNGLE.

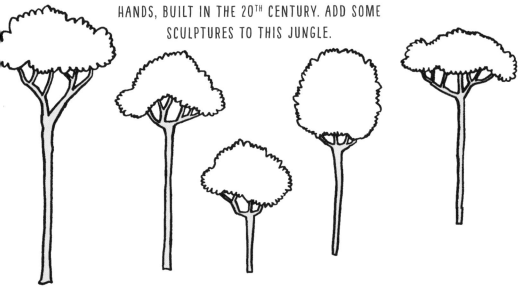

274.

NEAR VANCOUVER ISLAND, CANADA, YOU CAN TAKE A BOAT TRIP TO SEE ORCA, HUMPBACK WHALES, AND GRAY WHALES IN THE WILD. DRAW WHAT YOU MIGHT SEE THROUGH THESE BINOCULARS.

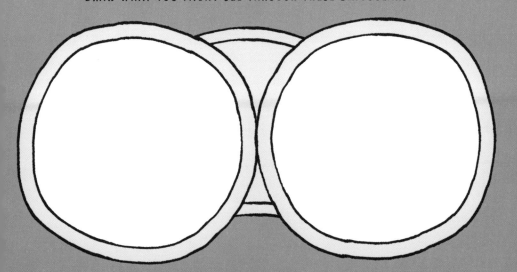

275.

NEWGRANGE IS A 5,200-YEAR-OLD TOMB IN IRELAND. ONE OF ITS CHAMBERS WAS CLEVERLY BUILT SO THAT IT ONLY LETS IN A SINGLE BEAM OF SUNLIGHT ON THE SHORTEST DAY OF THE YEAR. ADD A BEAM OF SUNLIGHT BRIGHTENING UP THIS ANCIENT ROOM.

276.

IN MADEIRA, PORTUGAL, TOURISTS DESCEND A MOUNTAIN BY TOBOGGANING DOWN A 1¼-MILE-LONG PATH. DRAW YOURSELF ON THIS TOBOGGAN AND MAKE IT LOOK LIKE IT'S SPEEDING DOWNHILL.

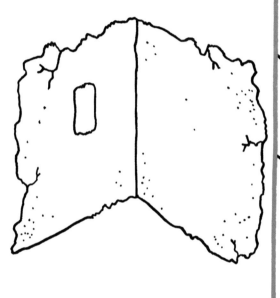

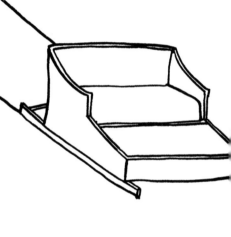

277.

THE HOBA METEORITE, IN NAMIBIA, LIES IN THE SAME SPOT IT LANDED WHEN IT FELL TO EARTH AROUND 80,000 YEARS AGO. A LOCAL FARMER DISCOVERED IT BY CHANCE IN 1920. WRITE A SENTENCE DESCRIBING HOW YOU'D FEEL IF YOU FOUND A METEORITE IN YOUR BACKYARD.

278.

IMAGINE THAT YOU'VE WON A TRIP TO ONE COUNTRY ON EACH CONTINENT (EXCEPT ANTARCTICA!). WHERE DO YOU CHOOSE TO GO, AND WHY?

AFRICA

SOUTH AMERICA

EUROPE

ASIA

NORTH AMERICA

AUSTRALIA & OCEANIA

279.

IF YOU VISIT ANOTHER COUNTRY, YOU MIGHT FIND FOODS THAT SEEM UNUSUAL TO YOU BUT ARE PERFECTLY NORMAL THERE, LIKE TUNA EYEBALLS IN JAPAN OR DRIED SHARK IN ICELAND. WHAT FOODS DO YOU EAT THAT A VISITOR FROM ABROAD MIGHT FIND STRANGE?

280.

AMA ARE JAPANESE WOMEN WHO DIVE DOWN TO THE SEABED, WITHOUT OXYGEN TANKS, TO COLLECT PEARLS, SEAFOOD, AND SHELLS TO SELL AT MARKETS. WHAT WOULD YOU COLLECT FROM THE BOTTOM OF THE SEA?

281.

THE PUERTO PRINCESA UNDERGROUND RIVER IN THE PHILIPPINES IS ONE OF THE WORLD'S LONGEST UNDERGROUND RIVERS. MAKE UP A CREATURE THAT WOULD LIVE IN AN UNDERGROUND RIVER.

282.

BLOOD FALLS IN ANTARCTICA LOOKS LIKE A WATERFALL OF BLOOD POURING DOWN AN ICY SLOPE. IT GETS ITS RED COLOR FROM IRON IN THE WATER. WRITE A STORY ABOUT BEING THE FIRST PERSON TO SEE IT.

283.

GLASS BEACH IN CALIFORNIA IS A SPARKLING BEACH OF SMOOTH GLASS PEBBLES FORMED FROM BROKEN BOTTLES THROWN AWAY YEARS AGO. DESIGN A POSTER TELLING PEOPLE NOT TO LITTER.

284.

THE WORLD'S LONGEST TUNNEL SLIDE IS AT THE ORBIT IN LONDON, ENGLAND. IT TAKES 40 SECONDS TO GO DOWN AND YOU CAN REACH SPEEDS OF 15 MILES PER HOUR. DESIGN ANOTHER TWISTY, INTERESTING SLIDE.

285.

MANY COUNTRIES HAVE NATIONAL PARKS, WHERE NATURAL OR HISTORICAL SITES ARE CARED FOR AND PRESERVED FOR THE FUTURE. IF YOU COULD TURN ANY AREA NEAR YOU INTO A NATIONAL PARK, WHERE WOULD IT BE, AND WHY?

286.

ACCORDING TO LEGEND, NOUNOU MOUNTAIN IN HAWAII IS ACTUALLY A GIANT THAT FELL ASLEEP AFTER EATING TOO MUCH, AND IS STILL SNOOZING. TURN THIS MOUNTAIN INTO A SLEEPING GIANT.

287.

THE GRAND MOSQUE AT DJENNÉ, MALI, IS THE WORLD'S BIGGEST MUD-BRICK BUILDING. EVERY APRIL, LOCALS REPAIR ANY DAMAGE TO IT WITH NEW LAYERS OF MUD. WHAT BUILDING NEAR YOU WOULD YOU GET YOUR LOCAL COMMUNITY TO REPAIR OR REDECORATE?

288.

A ROAD TRIP IS A VACATION WHERE PEOPLE DRIVE A LONG WAY OVER DAYS, WEEKS, OR EVEN MONTHS. WHERE WOULD YOUR DREAM ROAD TRIP START AND END, AND WHAT WOULD YOU SEE ALONG THE WAY?

289.

THE LONGEST RAILWAY LINE IN THE WORLD IS THE TRANS-SIBERIAN RAILWAY, AT 5,772 MILES. IT TRAVELS THE LENGTH OF RUSSIA FROM WEST TO EAST. DESIGN A FANCY TICKET TO RIDE IT.

290.

ABUNA YEMATA GUH, A CHURCH IN ETHIOPIA, IS HOME TO WALL PAINTINGS OVER 1,000 YEARS OLD. BUT TO REACH IT, VISITORS MUST CLIMB A SHEER, NARROW PATH WITH NO GUARDRAIL, RISKING A 650-FOOT DROP ON EITHER SIDE. WOULD YOU MAKE THE CLIMB?

291.

SAN FRANCISCO, CALIFORNIA, IS OFTEN SHROUDED IN FOG THAT BLOWS IN FROM THE PACIFIC OCEAN. THE FOG HAS A NAME: KARL! GIVE KARL A FRIENDLY FACE.

292.

ON FLIGHTS AROUND THE WORLD, YOU CAN LOOK OUT THE WINDOW AND SEE NATURAL AND MAN-MADE LANDMARKS FROM ABOVE. WHAT WOULD YOU MOST LIKE TO SEE FROM THE AIR?

293.

MOAI ARE HUGE STONE FIGURES ON EASTER ISLAND, IN CHILE, BUILT AROUND 500 YEARS AGO. WHAT'S ONE QUESTION YOU WOULD ASK THE PEOPLE WHO MADE THEM, IF YOU COULD?

294.

CUCKOO CLOCKS WERE INVENTED IN GERMANY, BUT ARE A COMMON SYMBOL OF SWITZERLAND. THESE WOODEN CLOCKS SEND OUT A MODEL CUCKOO BIRD WHICH CHIMES TO ANNOUNCE THE HOUR. DESIGN YOUR OWN CUCKOO CLOCK HERE.

295.

AT CHICHÉN ITZÁ, IN MEXICO, THERE'S A 1,100-YEAR-OLD PYRAMID DEDICATED TO THE MAYAN SNAKE GOD, KUKULCÁN. TWICE A YEAR, SUNLIGHT HITS ITS STEPS TO MAKE IT LOOK LIKE KUKULCÁN IS COMING DOWN THEM. DRAW A SNAKE SLITHERING DOWN THIS PYRAMID.

296.

OYMYAKON, RUSSIA, IS THE COLDEST PLACE WHERE PEOPLE LIVE ON EARTH, WITH AN AVERAGE TEMPERATURE OF -58°F. WRITE DOWN FIVE THINGS YOU WOULD WEAR OR DO TO KEEP WARM IF YOU LIVED THERE.

1. _____

_____

2. _____

_____

3. _____

_____

4. _____

_____

5. _____

_____

297.

IN LONDON, ENGLAND, PEOPLE CALLED "PEARLY KINGS AND QUEENS" RAISE MONEY FOR CHARITY WHILE WEARING CLOTHES COVERED WITH MOTHER-OF-PEARL BUTTONS. ADD A PATTERN OF SHINY BUTTONS TO THESE OUTFITS.

298.

IN THE PHILIPPINES, OLD MILITARY VEHICLES ARE USED AS PUBLIC TRANSPORATION. DRIVERS OF THESE "JEEPNEYS" DECORATE THEM IN BRIGHT, BOLD COLORS, AND SLOGANS. DESIGN YOUR OWN JEEPNEY HOWEVER YOU LIKE.

299.

IN PEMBROKESHIRE, WALES, CAMPERS CAN STAY IN A POD SHAPED LIKE AN ALIEN SPACESHIP. DESCRIBE OR DRAW WHAT THE INSIDE MIGHT LOOK LIKE.

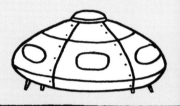

300.

SOME COUNTRIES HAVE A NATIONAL DANCE, SUCH AS THE ARGENTINE TANGO OR IRISH STEP DANCING. WHAT DANCE WOULD YOU LIKE TO LEARN?

301.

IN NARA, JAPAN, DEER HAVE BEEN SO WELL-TREATED FOR SO LONG THAT THEY ARE CALM AROUND PEOPLE, AND ROAM THE STREETS LOOKING FOR FOOD FROM TOURISTS. WHAT ANIMAL WOULD YOU WANT TO LIVE PEACEFULLY ALONGSIDE IF YOU COULD?

302.

THE GRAND BAZAAR IN ISTANBUL, TURKEY, IS A GIGANTIC INDOOR MARKET BUILT IN 1455. SHOPS THERE SELL EVERYTHING FROM LANTERNS AND CLOTH TO SPICES AND DYES. FILL THIS SHOP FRONT WITH COLORFUL GOODS FOR SALE.

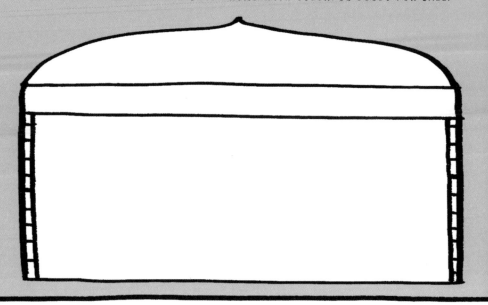

303.

ONE OF THE MOST DANGEROUS SEA JOURNEYS IN THE WORLD IS AROUND CAPE HORN, CHILE. WRITE A DIARY ENTRY ABOUT SAILING THROUGH ITS TERRIBLE STORMS AND HUGE WAVES.

304.

DIFFERENT PEOPLE HAVE DIFFERENT WAYS TO KEEP FROM GETTING BORED ON LONG JOURNEYS. WRITE DOWN FIVE THINGS YOU CAN DO TO KEEP YOURSELF ENTERTAINED WHILE TRAVELING.

1. _____

2. _____

3. _____

4. _____

5. _____

305.

THE SAGRADA FAMÍLIA IS A CATHEDRAL IN BARCELONA, SPAIN, KNOWN FOR ITS FANTASTICAL DESIGN. ADD SOME MORE UNUSUAL FEATURES TO THE SAGRADA FAMÍLIA.

306.

IN SCOTLAND, THE FIRST PERSON TO ENTER A HOUSE ON NEW YEAR'S DAY CARRIES A PIECE OF COAL FOR GOOD LUCK. MAKE UP ANOTHER NEW YEAR'S DAY TRADITION.

_____

_____

_____

_____

_____

307.

SNAKE ISLAND, OFF THE COAST OF BRAZIL, HAS NO PEOPLE, JUST POISONOUS SNAKES—LOTS AND LOTS OF THEM. DRAW A WARNING SIGN FOR THE BEACH.

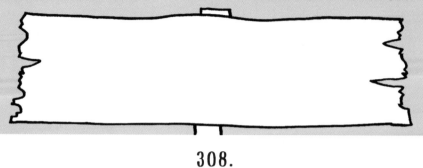

308.

IN THE AUSTRALIAN BUSH, WEARING A HAT WITH DANGLING CORKS CHASES AWAY FLIES AS YOU MOVE. ADD SOME MORE INTERESTING OBJECTS AROUND THIS HAT.

309.

SERENDIPITY 3 IS A RESTAURANT IN NEW YORK CITY THAT SELLS EXPENSIVE, EXTRAVAGANT FOOD, SUCH AS A $1,000 ICE CREAM SUNDAE WITH REAL GOLD ON IT. MAKE UP AND DRAW AN AMAZING DISH TO SERVE THERE.

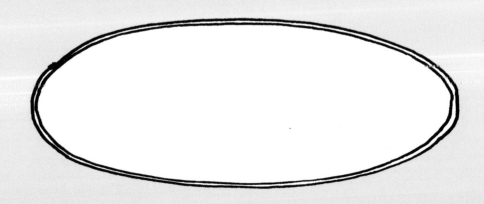

310.

THE SINGING RINGING TREE IN LANCASHIRE, ENGLAND, IS A TREE-SHAPED SCULPTURE MADE OF PIPES. WHEN THE WIND BLOWS THROUGH THE PIPES, IT PLAYS MUSIC. DESIGN YOUR OWN WINDBLOWN INSTRUMENT HERE.

311.

IN OKLAHOMA, IT'S ILLEGAL TO LET A DONKEY SLEEP IN YOUR BATHTUB AFTER 7:00 P.M. MAKE UP THREE MORE LAWS RELATING TO ANIMALS.

1. _____

_____

_____

2. _____

_____

_____

3. _____

_____

_____

312. THE URU PEOPLE OF BOLIVIA AND PERU LIVE ON FLOATING ISLANDS IN LAKE TITICACA. THEY MAKE THE ISLANDS AND THEIR HOUSES FROM TOTORA REEDS. DRAW YOUR OWN FLOATING ISLAND AND HOME HERE.

313. EVERY YEAR IN THE US, AT LEAST ONE LIVE TURKEY IS OFFICIALLY PARDONED BY THE PRESIDENT—SO IT DOESN'T END UP BEING THANKSGIVING DINNER. WRITE A SPEECH FOR THE TURKEY TO GIVE.

314. ON PALMYRA ATOLL IN THE PACIFIC OCEAN, IT'S HOT AND HUMID ALL YEAR. IF YOU HAD TO HAVE THE SAME WEATHER ALL THE TIME, WHAT WOULD YOU LIKE IT TO BE?

315. CROP CIRCLES ARE DESIGNS IN FIELDS FORMED BY FLATTENED CORN OR WHEAT. THEY HAVE APPEARED OFTEN IN ENGLAND. SOME SAY THEY'RE PRACTICAL JOKES—OTHERS THAT THEY'RE MORE MYSTERIOUS. ADD ANOTHER CROP CIRCLE DESIGN TO THIS FIELD.

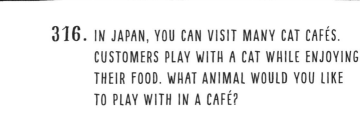

316. IN JAPAN, YOU CAN VISIT MANY CAT CAFÉS. CUSTOMERS PLAY WITH A CAT WHILE ENJOYING THEIR FOOD. WHAT ANIMAL WOULD YOU LIKE TO PLAY WITH IN A CAFÉ?

317.

A FAMOUS ALLEY IN STOCKHOLM, SWEDEN, IS ONLY 35 INCHES WIDE. MÅRTEN TROTZIGS GRÄND IS SUCH A TIGHT SQUEEZE THAT TWO PEOPLE CAN'T WALK SIDE BY SIDE. DESIGN A WAY FOR PEOPLE TO PASS EACH OTHER IN THIS ALLEY. YOU COULD ADD A BRIDGE, AN ELEVATOR, OR ANYTHING ELSE YOU CAN IMAGINE!

318.

IN VANUATU, HARVEST IS CELEBRATED BY YOUNG MEN JUMPING FROM HIGH STICK TOWERS WITH A VINE TIED TO THEIR ANKLES. THE VINE IS JUST THE RIGHT LENGTH TO STOP THEM FROM HITTING THE GROUND! DRAW A TOWER OF STICKS FOR THEM TO JUMP FROM.

319.

THE WINTER OLYMPIC GAMES OCCUR EVERY FOUR YEARS IN
A DIFFERENT CITY AROUND THE WORLD. WHICH THREE CHILLY
LOCATIONS WOULD YOU PICK FOR THE GAMES?

320.

SIX FLAGS GREAT ADVENTURE IN NEW JERSEY CALLS ITSELF THE
SECOND-LARGEST THEME PARK IN THE WORLD. IT COMBINES TRADITIONAL RIDES
WITH AN ANIMAL SAFARI PARK. DRAW AN AD FOR YOUR DREAM THEME PARK.

321.

PADDINGTON STATION IN LONDON, ENGLAND, HAS A STATUE OF PADDINGTON
BEAR. WHICH CHARACTER FROM A CHILDREN'S BOOK WOULD YOU
LIKE TO SEE AS A STATUE? WHERE SHOULD IT BE?

322.

IN CHINA, IT'S CONSIDERED POLITE TO REFUSE A GIFT UP TO THREE TIMES BEFORE TAKING IT. WHAT GIFT WOULD YOU FIND IT HARD TO REFUSE THREE TIMES?

323.

CHULLOS ARE TRADITIONAL HATS FROM THE ANDE MOUNTAINS, OFTEN MADE FROM ALPACA WOOL. SOME ARE KNITTED TIGHTLY ENOUGH TO HOLD WATER! ADD A BRIGHT DESIGN TO THIS CHULLO.

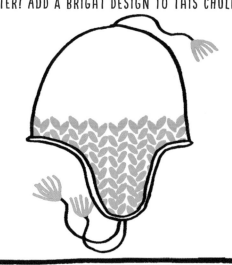

324.

SOMETIMES PEOPLE TRAVEL TO HELP WILDLIFE, SUCH AS VOLUNTEERING TO CARE FOR BABY SLOTHS OR RESCUED ELEPHANTS. IMAGINE YOU HAVE DONE SOMETHING SIMILAR. WRITE A MESSAGE HOME DESCRIBING YOUR EXPERIENCE.

325.

IN JAPAN, PEOPLE CAN BUY ALL SORTS OF THINGS FROM VENDING MACHINES, INCLUDING VEGETABLES AND EVEN FISH. FILL THIS VENDING MACHINE WITH UNEXPECTED ITEMS.

326.

AFTER A DUTCH SHIP WAS WRECKED OFF OF SOUTH AFRICA IN 1647, THE STRANDED SAILORS HAD TO EAT WHAT THEY COULD FIND OR TRADE, INCLUDING RHINOCEROS MEAT AND PENGUIN EGGS. MAKE UP A MENU FOR LOST TRAVELERS IN YOUR COUNTRY IF THERE WERE NO STORES.

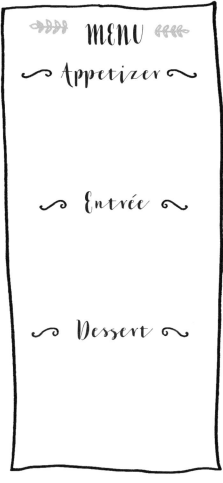

MENU

Appetizer

Entrée

Dessert

327.

THE MERCURE KAKADU CROCODILE HOTEL IN AUSTRALIA IS SHAPED LIKE A GIANT CROCODILE SPRAWLING OVER THE LAND. DRAW A CROCODILE FAMILY ON VACATION.

328.

IN DEPOK, INDONESIA, PEOPLE TAKE PART IN PALM-TREE-CLIMBING COMPETITIONS. DESIGN A CERTIFICATE FOR THE WINNER.

329.

IN BALTIMORE, MARYLAND, IT'S ILLEGAL TO TAKE A LION TO THE CINEMA. MAKE UP A STORY THAT MIGHT HAVE LED TO THIS LAW BEING PASSED.

330.

MACHU PICCHU IS AN INCA RUIN IN PERU, BUILT AROUND 600 YEARS AGO. VISITORS REACH IT VIA A WINDING MOUNTAIN PATH FROM THE NEAREST VILLAGE. DRAW A ZIGZAG PATH UP THIS MOUNTAIN, CONNECTING THE VILLAGE TO MACHU PICCHU.

331.

LUNDY ISLAND, OFF THE COAST OF DEVON, ENGLAND,
HAS 15 TIMES AS MANY PUFFINS AS HUMANS.
DRAW YOURSELF AMONG THE PUFFINS.

332.

WHEN YOU ENTER OR LEAVE A COUNTRY, YOU SOMETIMES GET A STAMP IN
YOUR PASSPORT. EVERY COUNTRY HAS A DIFFERENT STAMP DESIGN. FILL THIS
PASSPORT WITH MADE-UP STAMPS FROM AROUND THE WORLD.

333.

THE SMALL TOWN OF GUNDAGAI, IN AUSTRALIA, HAS A SCULPTURE OF A DOG SITTING ON A LARGE LUNCH BOX. DESIGN A SCULPTURE BASED ON TWO THINGS YOU CAN SEE RIGHT NOW.

334.

DO YOU KNOW WHAT YOUR COUNTRY LOOKS LIKE FROM ABOVE? DRAW IT FROM MEMORY—THEN CHECK A GLOBE OR ATLAS TO COMPARE!

335.

THE VILLAGE OF TE WAIROA IN NEW ZEALAND WAS BURIED IN MUD AND ASH AFTER A VOLCANIC EXPLOSION IN 1886. THE TOPS OF THE HOUSES ARE STILL VISIBLE AND A POPULAR TOURIST ATTRACTION. DRAW THE PART OF THIS HOUSE THAT'S BURIED UNDERGROUND.

336.

VISITORS TO BLARNEY CASTLE, IN IRELAND, SOMETIMES KISS A PART OF ITS WALL CALLED THE BLARNEY STONE. LEGEND HAS IT THAT THIS GIVES YOU THE ABILITY TO SPEAK SKILLFULLY AND PERSUASIVELY. WHAT WOULD YOU USE THIS ABILITY FOR?

337.

VAADHOO, THE MALDIVES, IS HOME TO THE "SEA OF STARS," WHERE GLOWING PLANKTON MAKES THE WATER BRIGHT BLUE AT NIGHT. COLOR THIS WATER THE BRIGHTEST BLUE YOU CAN.

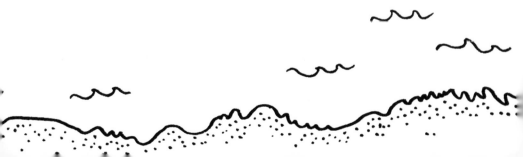

338.

HASHIMA ISLAND, IN JAPAN, WAS SUDDENLY ABANDONED IN 1974
AFTER ITS COAL MINES, WHERE MOST RESIDENTS WORKED, CLOSED
DOWN. WITH NO ONE ABOUT, NATURE HAS RETURNED TO THE ISLAND.
DRAW A FOREST COVERING THESE EMPTY BUILDINGS.

339.

CONSTELLATIONS ARE GROUPS OF STARS IN THE NIGHT SKY THAT PEOPLE
HAVE USED THROUGHOUT HISTORY TO FIND THEIR WAY AROUND.
THEY'RE LIKE DOT-TO-DOT PUZZLES, FORMING PATTERNS OR PICTURES.
TURN THESE STARS INTO NEW CONSTELLATIONS.

340.

AT THE PIKE PLACE MARKET IN SEATTLE, WASHINGTON, FISHMONGERS ENTERTAIN THE CROWDS BY THROWING GIANT FISH TO EACH OTHER, BEFORE WRAPPING THEM UP FOR SALE. DRAW THE FISH THAT'S BEEN THROWN BY THESE FISHMONGERS.

341.

BONBON-LAND IN COPENHAGEN, DENMARK, IS A THEME PARK OF GROSS-SOUNDING CANDIES, INCLUDING SEAGULL DROPPINGS AND EARWAX. INVENT THREE MORE CANDIES ON THIS THEME.

1. —————————————

——————————————

2. —————————————

——————————————

3. —————————————

——————————————

342.

THE VICTORIA FALLS BRIDGE CONNECTS TWO COUNTRIES: ZAMBIA AND ZIMBABWE. IF YOU COULD CONNECT YOUR COUNTRY BY A BRIDGE TO ANY OTHER COUNTRY IN THE WORLD, WHICH WOULD IT BE?

——————————————

——————————————

——————————————

——————————————

——————————————

343.

WATER PUPPETS ARE A VIETNAMESE TRADITION. HIDDEN PERFORMERS CONTROL WOODEN PUPPETS WITH BAMBOO RODS, TO ACT OUT FOLK STORIES IN POOLS OF WATER. FILL THIS WATER THEATER WITH PUPPETS.

344.

LEGEND HAS IT THAT THE FIRST MARGHERITA PIZZA WAS TOPPED WITH BASIL, MOZZARELLA CHEESE, AND TOMATO, TO REPRESENT THE GREEN, WHITE, AND RED OF ITALY'S FLAG. IF YOU MADE A PIZZA THE COLORS OF YOUR COUNTRY'S FLAG, WHAT INGREDIENTS WOULD YOU WANT TO USE?

345.

IN CAPPADOCIA, TURKEY, TOURISTS TAKE TO THE SKIES IN HUNDREDS
OF COLORFUL HOT-AIR BALLOONS. ADD DECORATIVE BALLOONS TO
FLOAT THESE BASKETS, THEN FILL THEM WITH TOURISTS.

346.

TAKE A ROAD TRIP THROUGH AUSTRALIA, AND YOU MIGHT SEE ONE OF MANY
"BIG THINGS." THESE GIANT ROADSIDE SCULPTURES INCLUDE A KOALA,
A SHRIMP, AND A BANANA. DESIGN A NEW "BIG THING" TO GO WITH THEM.

347.

YUNESSUN SPA RESORT, IN JAPAN, FEATURES HOT BATHS WITH A DIFFERENCE: YOU CAN BATHE IN COFFEE, TEA, OR EVEN NOODLE BROTH! WHAT FOOD WOULD YOU PICK TO TAKE A DIP IN?

348.

THAMES TOWN IS AN AREA OF SHANGHAI, CHINA, THAT LOOKS EXACTLY LIKE A TYPICAL ENGLISH VILLAGE. IMAGINE THAT A SECTION OF YOUR HOMETOWN WAS THEMED AROUND ANOTHER COUNTRY. WHICH COUNTRY WOULD YOU CHOOSE, AND WHAT WOULD YOU CALL THE AREA?

349.

PEOPLE ON THE TINY SPANISH ISLAND OF LA GOMERA CAN COMMUNICATE IN A LANGUAGE MADE ENTIRELY OF WHISTLES. WHAT WOULD YOU SAY TO A FRIEND IN WHISTLE LANGUAGE RIGHT NOW?

350.

IF YOU COULD VISIT ANY REAL PLACE YOU KNOW FROM A BOOK, MOVIE, OR TV SHOW, WHAT WOULD IT BE, AND WHY?

_____

_____

_____

_____

_____

_____

_____

351. HENLEY-ON-TODD, IN AUSTRALIA, IS HOME TO A BOAT RACE WITH A DIFFERENCE: THERE'S NO WATER! TEAMS OF CONTESTANTS CARRY THEIR BOATS AROUND A DRY COURSE, WITH THEIR LEGS POKING OUT OF THE BOTTOM. DRAW YOURSELF AND A TEAM OF FRIENDS RACING THIS BOAT.

352.
COLOMBIA IS HOME TO OVER 3,000 SPECIES OF BUTTERFLY. ADD ANOTHER BY COLORING IN THIS ONE.

353.

BIG TEX IS THE 55-FOOT-TALL "WORLD'S LARGEST COWBOY"—A WOODEN STATUE WHO WELCOMES VISITORS TO THE TEXAS STATE FAIR. COLOR IN TEX HOWEVER YOU LIKE.

354.

TORONTO, CANADA, HOSTS THE ANNUAL WORLD ROCK, PAPER, SCISSORS CHAMPIONSHIPS. THINK YOU'VE GOT WHAT IT TAKES? USE THIS TABLE TO RECORD WINS AND LOSSES WITH A FRIEND. BEST OF THREE WINS!

PLAYER 1	PLAYER 2

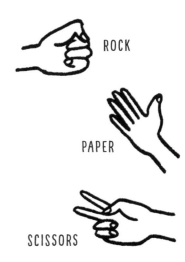

ROCK

PAPER

SCISSORS

355.

MANY PLACES AROUND THE WORLD HAVE LIGHTHOUSES BUILT ON ROCKS NEAR THE SHORE TO WARN SHIPS OF DANGER OR GUIDE THEM INTO PORT. DRAW A LIGHTHOUSE ON THESE ROCKS.

356.

IN THE PHILIPPINES, YOU CAN GET CHEESE AND COCONUT ICE CREAM. IN CHINA, RED BEAN ICE CREAM IS POPULAR. MAKE UP FIVE NEW ICE CREAM FLAVORS.

1. _____

_____

2. _____

_____

3. _____

_____

4. _____

_____

5. _____

_____

357.

"FUGU" IS A KIND OF PUFFER FISH SERVED AS A DELICACY IN JAPAN. IT'S SO POISONOUS THAT SOME PEOPLE HAVE DIED FROM EATING IT—BUT IT'S SAID TO BE VERY TASTY. WOULD YOU WANT TO TRY IT?

358.

A NOMAD IS SOMEONE WHO TRAVELS THE LAND, LIVING IN MANY DIFFERENT PLACES. THE NOMADIC LIFESTYLE OFTEN DEPENDS ON FOLLOWING HERDS OF ANIMALS. WHAT WOULD BE GOOD AND BAD ABOUT LIVING IN THIS WAY?

359.

CHESS BOXING STARTED IN BERLIN, GERMANY, AND IS NOW PLAYED AROUND THE WORLD. CONTESTANTS HAVE SIX ROUNDS OF CHESS AND FIVE ROUNDS OF BOXING. WHAT WACKY CONTEST WOULD YOU MAKE FROM TWO DIFFERENT GAMES OR SPORTS?

360.

THE HALL OF MIRRORS IS IN THE PALACE OF VERSAILLES, NEAR PARIS, FRANCE. AN ENTIRE WALL IS COVERED WITH MIRRORS. FILL THIS WALL WITH MIRRORS OF ALL SHAPES AND SIZES, THEN DRAW WHAT'S REFLECTED IN THEM.

361.

MANY EUROPEAN COUNTRIES HAVE TOWNS SURROUNDED BY STONE WALLS. THE WALLS WERE MOSTLY BUILT IN MEDIEVAL TIMES, AS A WAY TO KEEP THE TOWNSPEOPLE SAFE. DRAW A TOWN INSIDE THIS WALL.

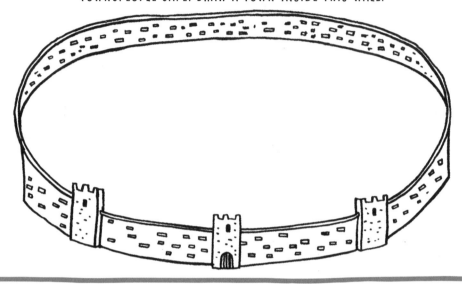

362.

AT HOTEL MESÓN DE JOBITO, IN MEXICO, VISITORS REPORT SPOOKY SIGHTINGS OF GHOSTLY MINERS AND THE SOUND OF HORSES' HOOVES. DESCRIBE SPENDING THE NIGHT THERE ... IF YOU DARE!

363.

IMAGINE YOU ARE IN CHARGE OF PICKING YOUR COUNTRY'S NEW CAPITAL CITY. WHICH CITY DO YOU CHOOSE, AND WHY?

364.

SINGER-SONGWRITER DOLLY PARTON HAS HER OWN THEME PARK IN TENNESSEE: DOLLYWOOD! IF YOU HAD A THEME PARK ABOUT YOURSELF, WHAT WOULD BE IN IT?

365.

IMAGINE YOU'RE TAKING A TRIP IN A FOREIGN COUNTRY. WRITE A POSTCARD TO A FRIEND BACK HOME. DESCRIBE WHERE YOU ARE AND WHAT ADVENTURES YOU'VE HAD.

First American Edition 2022
Kane Miller, A Division of EDC Publishing

Copyright © 2022 Quarto Publishing plc

For information contact:
Kane Miller, A Division of EDC Publishing
5402 S 122nd E Avenue, Tulsa, OK 74146
www.kanemiller.com
www.myubam.com

Library of Congress Control Number: 2021950007

ISBN: 978-1-68464-451-3

Manufactured in Huizhou City, Guangdong, China. TT032022

1 2 3 4 5 6 7 8 9 10

MIX
Paper from
responsible sources
FSC® C016973
FSC
www.fsc.org